What people

Num

Numerology: Dancing the Spirals of Time is not just another volume full of number and letter charts. Far deeper and more profound than that, it's an exploration of the rhythms and cycles of numbers as they affect our lives, from daily activities to the arc of a lifetime's spiritual path. Dig into the ways the patterns of time affect you via your conception and birth dates, with nuances of day, month, year, and century – yes, they all matter. Delve into the connections between given and chosen names and the direction of your life path. What goes around, comes around, so let Elen Sentier take you on a journey of discovery through the spiralling mysteries of the numbers. I really enjoyed it, learned new things even though I've been studying numerology for years.
Laura Perry, author of *Ariadne's Thread: Awakening the Wonders of the Ancient Minoans in Our Modern Lives*

A fascinating and enjoyable read revealing the mysteries of numbers to the uninitiated. It even taught this numerical scientist a thing or two!
Brendan Howlin, author of The *Handbook of Urban Druidry* and *The Urban Ovate*

To help you make up your mind about buying and reading this book, let me quote one line from it that says it all: "Numbers dance the patterns of life and of time". Elen Sentier's book is not only about numbers it is about Life and how numbers play their sacred role in the miracle that is Life. If you are not convinced yet, here are two more lines: "We old ones have kept our ways hidden in plain sight for over two thousand years now" and "As far as I can discover neither Eliade nor Harner ever came to speak with us old ones in Britain" – when one of the old ones,

from a family line of cunning folk, is willing to share her deep ancestral knowing and medicine teachings in a book – you pre-order your copy!!
Imelda Almqvist, international teacher of sacred art and shamanism, author of *Natural Born Shamans: A Spiritual Toolkit for Life* and *SACRED ART, A Hollow Bone for Spirit: Where Shamanism Meets Art*

If you are interested in learning more about numerology then this is the book to read. Elen Sentier takes you on a journey using her own stories and years of experience to help explain the meaning behind it all. Numbers, balances and patterns and how they all relate to each other, and to you as a person. Fascinating for anyone that wants to delve into number magic.
Rachel Patterson, author of the *Kitchen Witchcraft* series, *Witchcraft into the Wilds & Animal Magic*

In her usual engaging and soulful way, Elen Sentier explores a complex and ancient guide to identity and destiny that comes out of an awareness now radical for us: that the universe is actually an orderly place where number, shape, pattern and relationship coincide, all mirroring each other.
Jay Ramsey, author and poet

This is the most reader-friendly numerology book we've come across! Numerologists use numbers to discover how people work, what makes them tick, because numbers are a code for life. The numbers of one's birth provide the clues to the pattern of that incarnation. Knowing the pattern enables us to bring more of it to light, to consciousness, and so helps us grow. Bringing one's self to consciousness can be very difficult and painful, but until we do we have no chance of being whole. Becoming whole helps the whole planet and everything that lives and breathes and has its being thereon. This is an innovative and inspirational book.
Capall Bann, Amazon

Numerology

Dancing the Spirals of Time

Numerology

Dancing the Spirals of Time

Elen Sentier

MOON
BOOKS

Winchester, UK
Washington, USA

First published by Moon Books, 2019
Moon Books is an imprint of John Hunt Publishing Ltd., No. 3 East Street, Alresford
Hampshire SO24 9EE, UK
office1@jhpbooks.net
www.johnhuntpublishing.com
www.moon-books.net

For distributor details and how to order please visit the 'Ordering' section on our website.

Text copyright: Elen Sentier 2018

ISBN: 978 1 78279 656 5
978 1 78279 655 8 (ebook)
Library of Congress Control Number: 2018931098

A CIP catalogue record for this book is available from the British Library.

Design: Stuart Davies

Printed and bound by CPI Group (UK) Ltd, Croydon, CR0 4YY, UK

We operate a distinctive and ethical publishing philosophy in
all areas of our business, from our global network of authors to
production and worldwide distribution.

Contents

Contents

To Paul, for 45 years of exploring the bright darkness
with me ...

Prologue

Numbers are our connection to the universe.

They're a shorthand code which seems likely to be understood throughout the universe. Scientists at SETI – Search for Extra-Terrestrial Intelligence – send out messages formed of numbers to the rest of the universe in the hope of getting an answer. Numerologists use them to help people discover what makes them tick. Numbers are a code which all of life, the universe and everything uses.

This book is about the significance of your birth and name numbers and how knowing them helps you relate to the Earth, the solar system, galaxy and cosmos. As you find what these numbers mean for you, *and* how to work with them, you'll feel more and more empowered. The book doesn't give you a set of didactic interpretations – that would mean you'd have to fit yourself into my box and my ideas (dreadful thought! LOL), but it does give you basic concepts which have stood the tests of time. And, more than that, it offers you ways and means to find out what the numbers mean for yourself. That is real and empowering. You will find you can use the techniques in all other parts of your life as well as numerology.

And remember, no one person ever has all the answers, so don't treat any book (including this one!) as the definitive lore. Each of us gives what we can at the time we write. The great Natural Philosopher, Albert Newton, said of himself that he was just a pebble on the sea-shore and that out there is the vast ocean. If he, genius that he was, was a pebble then the rest of us might be grains of sand ... but, we're all necessary, including you.

Enjoy your dance through the spiral of Time.

Using This Book

I'd better begin by saying there's no easy table of answers and meanings in this book! There are no formulas for interpreting your numerology, to learn this stuff you have to actually do it rather than learning somebody else's – in this case mine – script. Add in to that that my script is only where I am at the moment. I began playing and learning with numbers when I was eight years old, reading some of my Dad's books and asking him about it; so that means I've been doing this for sixty+ years to date, and I still learn more each time I do somebody's numbers with them.

Thirty-odd years ago one of my psychology teachers told us all this story …

'Once upon a time there was this tree-family who had a baby tree-girl. They adored her and wanted only the best for her, so they fed her the very best apple-tree food they could get. But she was a difficult tree, didn't grow properly, had lots of problems, was often ill and miserable, and didn't understand properly what went on around her in her family.

Then, one day, this wizard came walking through the wood where she lived. He saw the young tree girl, now near grown into a full tree woman, but still having lots of difficulties. He came to her, sat down beside her. He spent a little while hunting in his carry-sack and then brought out a beautiful coloured flask. 'Would you like a drink of this?' he asked her. She took the flask, sniffed it, it smelled good so she took a sip, it tasted good so she took another, soon she'd drunk nearly half the flask. 'Ooooo!' she said, looking around her, 'everything looks a bit different, brighter, more cheerful. Oh, and isn't that birdsong lovely. And look at the colour of those flowers.' She continued to look about her, noticing the differences she was seeing and hearing and smelling and tasting and feeling.

'What's happened?' she asked the wizard. 'Well,' he began, 'you see my dear, your parents thought you were an apple tree. That's what they are, so they automatically thought you were the same. But you're not, you're an orange tree. So all these years they've been giving you apple-tree food, and all these years it's been slowly poisoning you. I just gave you a drink of orange-tree food.' The tree-girl clapped her branches in delight, 'I feel so much better! I can see more clearly now, and I know what I see much better than I did before.'

The wizard smiled. 'Of course you do. Now, what you need to do is to make sure you eat the proper orange-tree food, so you get properly nourished. It may be a bit difficult to convince your parents of this, but you must persevere, they'll get it in the end.'

'Oh, I will! I will!' said the orange-tree girl. And she did, so she's now a happy tree-woman ... and is being very careful to find out what her own tree-children are, so she doesn't feed them the wrong food.'

Are you getting that? It really is important. So many of us are like the orange-tree girl. The people around us have, often with the very best of intentions, fed us the wrong food so our feeling, thinking, and intuitive selves have been starved and poisoned, and possibly our physical bodies too. We do our best to please those around us. We try hard to conform to what they tell us is "right", so we twist ourselves, maybe even cut off bits of our heels and toes to try to fit our foot into someone else's glass slipper, not realising that every single one of us is different.

So, if I were to give you a definitive set of rules I would be trying to make you all into clones of me, like the apple-tree parents tried to do to their orange-tree daughter. Ye gods! One of me is quite enough for Mother Earth to handle, she doesn't need any more, thank you very much. Instead I'm offering you the guidelines and concepts that have worked well for me, and that have grown in me through doing the work.

Another of my teachers said a thing that I've found very profound, 'Evil is often inappropriate good' ... ponder on that. It lines up well with one of Dad's favourite adages, 'Human beings are worse than cats at change!' and with T.S. Eliot's, 'Human beings cannot bear very much reality' from his poem Burnt Norton. Ponder on all of these, they really do help you find your own way through the wonderful spiral of time that our numbers can reveal.

What I'm offering you here are the results of my sixty-odd years of work and play with numerology, what the numbers have shown me. I've been fortunate enough to have many people to work with, who wanted me to help them explore their numbers. This process has shown me that these concepts really do work with other people. So, take what the book gives you and work with the ideas for yourself... you'll take it all further still.

Some Basic Concepts

To work with your numbers, it's really useful to get some basic concepts into your bones. They really are basic, and integral to working with numbers, and they pretty well encapsulate our old ways. They are ...

Asking
Listening
Befriending
Exchange

For us in the old ways, everything is animate, everything has the breath of life-spirit (where the word animate comes from), and is conscious. Even the fridge, the car, the mobile phone and the laptop have consciousness and the spirit of life. We human animals are not separate from the rest of creation, in fact we're made of every atom and molecule in creation. When we die, our bodies – the shell for our spirit, our spacesuit for living on Planet Earth – go back into those atoms and may well soon become part of a cabbage, virus, cat, car, road, train, or anything in their next incarnation. Those atoms hold memory too, so if we can learn how to contact that memory, we can learn about other things that are not part of us now. All the spirits of all of those other beasties and plants, like cats and worms and hedgehogs and trees as well as microbes and bacteria and viruses, are all older than us humans. We are the youngest species on Planet Earth. Our species, and our spirits, have only been around on Planet Earth for perhaps three million years, so everything else is older than us and, in all of the old ways all around the world, the younger learns from their elders.

So we ask everything – like we ask the car what's wrong and why she won't start this morning; and it's amazing what you learn by doing that! Even if your neighbours and family think you're right off the wall!

And, having asked, we listen to everything – like the car, or the cat, or even which cauliflower to buy for dinner.

And we befriend everything. We don't get all scared and terrified, even when whatever-it-is appears to us with green hairy teeth, bad breath and a load of attitude! As we speak with it, we learn if it's a spirit that wishes to help us or maybe one that needs our help. Or maybe it's a wretched, miserable, angry thoughtform, created by a wretched, miserable, angry, mean, pissed-off and frightened human being. And if it's the latter it most certainly needs our help.

Thoughtforms are like grumpy, sulky teenagers with lousy parents who've never taken proper care of them. They don't know what to do with themselves so they go round screwing things up for other people. The bad parents of the thoughtforms are the wretched people who thought them into existence in the first place, through their fears. They are born out of hate and fear, like fear of dogs or spiders; hating immigrants or black people or Jews; hating the person who got promoted when you thought it should be you; fear of not being loved (that's a huge one which most people suffer from!); fear of failure; fear of death even. I'm sure you can add to the list for yourself. These thoughtforms need help to go back into their component spirit-atoms, so they can stop being in the horrid situation the person who "thought" them has imprisoned them in.

So for us, everything, every single thing, is our friend. They help us and we help them – even horrid thoughtforms!

And that brings us to the principle of exchange; this is the fourth fundamental in our old ways. We always exchange ... you give me, I give you. That exchange might be physical things, help with something, or it might be that I've nothing you need so I give you "exchange-money" that you can swap with someone else later on. That's what money is, a means of exchange. It's not a commodity to be hoarded and grasped in a greedy way, although that is what we've turned it into now.

Our ways revolve around asking, listening, befriending and exchange.

We do this with everything, everything in thisworld and everything in otherworld too. And that's how we work with our numbers too.

Kenning: knowing in your bones

The well-known word "shaman" means "one who knows", but what is this *knowing*?

Take this scenario ... if someone throws a bucket of water over you, you *know* you are wet. It has nothing to do with belief, or with thinking, there's no "perhaps" about it, it's nobody's opinion, you didn't need to go to evening classes, or read it in a book, or go on a workshop, or look it up on Google. It's quite simple, you're wet! And you *know* it!

In Britain, we call this sort of knowing, *kenning*. You may have heard of it in the old song, "D'ye ken John Peel" where the word "ken" is used instead of know. The word comes from the Old Norse verb *kenna* "know, recognise; perceive, feel; show; teach", this expresses very well what I'm talking about here.

It's worth exploring the word ken, it gives you more of an idea how to work. The word is like daydreaming, far-fetching (as Ursula le Guin describes it), going beyond the ordinary and the obvious. It enables you to stretch yourself, stretch your boundaries, think outside the box and that is where creativity lies. If you learn to ken, with all its deeper meanings, then you no longer run on the tramlines of everyday normality.

The word has lasted, and is still known, through the expression *beyond one's ken*, meaning beyond the scope of one's knowledge and this, too, is a pretty good translation. The modern verb *to ken* survives in the Scottish language and some English dialects, Modern Scots uses *tae ken* meaning to know, and *kent* meaning knew or known in the past tense. The word is known in all sorts of places round the world. Old Norse *kenna*, modern Icelandic *kenna*, Swedish *känna*, Danish *kende*, Norwegian *kjenne* or *kjenna*. In Europe there's Old Frisian *kenna*, *kanna*, Old Saxon *kennian*, Dutch *kennen*, Old High German *chennan*, Middle High German and modern German *kennen*, and Gothic *kannjan*. The Proto-Germanic *kannjanan* comes from *kunnanan* meaning to know how to. In Afrikaans *ken* means to be acquainted with and to know, while *kennis* means knowledge. They all come from the same Proto-Indo-European root as the Modern English word *know*, and are all similar to the Old English word *cennan*.

Through the old ways, we're bringing the word back into use, back into the light again. The old ways are indeed beyond the scope of modern everyday knowledge. They carry the intimations of canny and uncanny, surreal, supernatural, shrewd, and prudent, all of which are pretty vital concepts in any work with spirit, and numbers. It's well time we expanded our vocabulary again to include such lovely and deep-meaning words.

To ken and kenning are also about euphemisms, re-wording, ambiguity, insinuation, innuendo and equivocation. These are ways to suggest rather than state unequivocally; they are ambiguous and circuitous, like circumlocution which is about being oblique, convoluted, and roundabout. The old ways of Britain are like this, we rarely go at anything straight but tend to sidle up to it, and we riddle worse than Zen poetry. To know, like the shaman knows – to ken – is to learn to read between lines, see round corners, gestalt, and never take anything straight.

All this really does help you get a full, deep and vibrant-coloured picture of everything. For example, Old Norse poets might replace the word for "sword", with "wound-hoe". Now, for me, that is seriously wow! I get such a different picture from the word wound-hoe, it tells me and shows me so much more of what happened, I can feel it in my body as well as see it in my mind's eye.

Our old British ways work like that. We come at things sideways out of the shadows so that we evoke deep meanings far beyond the simple word-name for something. Riddling helps get you out of your box, it goes deep and makes many connections which help you become integrated rather than compartmentalised into separate and disconnected segments. Our numbers, and the patterns they show us, help us to integrate ourselves.

Duality: creation unfinished, always in process

Long ago I read in one of Ursula le Guin's books a little mantram that people on that faraway world said to greet the sun and the new day: "... *praise then creation unfinished*" and I've loved it ever since. For me, perhaps for many of us, creation never ends despite all the Big Bang theories: for me, the universe breathes, is always breathing in and out, expanding and contracting as our lungs do with each breath we take. It never stops, and it never began, but has always been doing this. Roger Penrose's diagram of implosion/explosion does actually show this, but the scientists haven't got the maths together for that as yet. That's quite reasonable for me, I can't see why we should expect to know everything, instantly, all at once. I've been watching cutting edge physics (through my scientist-husband) for over forty years now and it seems that several of the world's top physicists are working towards something like the "breathing" idea. We'll see how it goes.

From when I was a baby, still sleeping in my cot, I used to be very easy to get to bed because, as I fell asleep, or rather in what they call the hypnogogic state before we actually sleep, I would have this experience. I would be lying in bed and I would feel my body become infinitely huge, I was filled with stars and galaxies all swirling inside me then, after a little time, I would feel myself become infinitely small, the tiniest dot at the centre of the huge swirling mass of stars. Then it would change back again to me being infinitely huge, and so on, I would cycle between hugeness and smallness, it was a slow process, like breathing. I loved it.

One day, Dad asked me why I so enjoyed going to bed so I told him about it. He smiled, 'I do that too,' he said, 'it's fun, isn't it?' It was so good that he knew, understood, didn't dismiss me and even experienced those things himself; it meant I didn't need to stuff my kennings to remain acceptable. Not until I went to school, then I had to, or I got laughed at and shunned for being weird. Yes, you have to learn to hide so you can work and be acceptable in the everyday world as well as with otherworld –learning about your numbers helps.

Old Ways: Hiding in Plain Sight

I was born on Dartmoor and grew up on Exmoor; my parents, family and the old ones in the villages where I grew up led me into the old ways of Britain. My mother's mother was a witch from the Isle of Man, and my father was a cyfarwydd (taleweaver) and awenydd (British shaman) who lived in Devon so I was born into an old family of cunning folk. I pass on the old ways through books on British native shamanism and in the magic/mystery/romance novels; I also offer training in the old British ways.

I'm a wilderness woman at heart, couldn't cope with living in a village let alone a town or city, so I live with my cats, husband and a host of wildlife in the back of beyond, a mile from a small secondary road, in the Welsh Marches. It's a magical twilight place, between two countries and between two worlds.

We British are an ancient people, current archaeology tells us there've been human beings living interesting, complex and sophisticated lives here in Britain for at least one million years. Not sophisticated as we think of it nowadays, not mobile phones and cars, not three or four jobs to try to afford the lifestyle but be unable to know our children. The old ones from way back then lived good lives, with plenty of time for pondering and thinking. Don't get the old-fashioned, and wrong, impression that life before farming was "nasty, brutish and short", it wasn't, far from it. Our hunter-gatherer ancestors worked perhaps 10-15 hours a week to get excellent nourishing food, plus the materials for clothing, tools, homes, everything they needed to live, and for art – look up the Swimming Reindeer at the British Museum website.

Figure 1: Swimming Reindeer

How many hours a week do you have to work now? And could you craft anything as exquisite as that? It's about 14,000 years old, from before the end of the last Ice Age and carved from a mammoth's tusk. Finds like this show us our ancient ancestors were intelligent people who thought deeply and whose minds were full of imagination; and they had far more time to discover and enjoy themselves than most of us do now.

Such people were mature, far more than most of us nowadays because they understood, and *knew in their bones*, how to *work-with* the Earth, how to be a part of the wholeness of Earth. Nowadays, many people feel they must control their environment, fight the planet – like the silly "Dangerous Planet" stuff we get on TV. Our ancestors knew the Earth as mother and friend, not something to be fought with and feared.

Each group and tribe had a thriving society too, but without all the problems we've built for ourselves through our concepts of ownership, hierarchy, and progress. They had no ladders of hierarchy that needed to be climbed to stay alive or to enhance one's ego, or gain enough money to maintain a lifestyle. The idea that any of us can "own" anything appeared with farming between 6 to 10 thousand years ago. Before that, we knew we owned nothing although we might be guardians of some things during our lifetime.

Since the advent of farming we've become extremely good at greed, theft, fighting, competitiveness, class, race and gender discrimination, hierarchy (I'm better than you!), and war – all because we believe in "ownership". Farming, with its relatively bad diet and the excruciating labour needed to produce and maintain that diet, led to our modern diseases of arthritis, diabetes, cancers, heart and cholesterol problems, obesity, and other conditions that frighten us now. I must admit I wonder why anyone wanted to adopt farming as a way of living. It feels far more like we made a big mistake and went the wrong way about it altogether.

But, that said, we're here now and we need to learn how to remake our attitudes so we can again connect with nature and our mother-planet, the Earth, and with everything else in the universe too. Which brings me again to knowing and working with our numbers and their incredible spiral patterns which can help us reconnect.

I first began playing with numbers when I was about seven years old. I watched Dad, asked what he was doing and he showed me. Dad would also take me out walking in the dark, especially when the moon wasn't up because that's when you can see the stars really well. He would explain about constellations, and what stars were made of, how they got born and how they die. And he'd tell me the old stories connected with them too. Back in the 1950s, on Dartmoor and Exmoor, there was very little light pollution so we could easily see the river of stars that is the Milky Way flowing overhead, with the Hunter (we call him Gwyn ap Nudd) striding along beside the river. With his pack of white, red-eyed, red-eared dogs, Gwyn is also the soul-catcher; he herds the souls across the river as they pass from thisworld to otherworld. In autumn, around the time of the Hunter's Moon, you can hear Gywn's dogs at twilight, like a skein of geese flying over.

Our old ways come down to us from prehistoric times through old stories, traditions, dances, songs, habits and ways of life; they're passed down through families and villages as they were to me. Of course, they've grown and changed as we have, over the centuries and millennia, as we have changed the face and the skin of Planet Earth with our farming, population growth, light pollution, global warming, everything we've done to try to make things easier for ourselves. In consequence, the rituals we do now are different to those our ancestors of a million, half a million, a thousand or even a hundred years ago. This happens everywhere, to all peoples, and it's a good thing. We need to include everything that happens to us now, not exclude it because our umpteen-times great-grand-parent didn't do it. For instance, the patterns the Navajo weavers use continually grow and change: at one point about a hundred years ago, they chose to incorporate the swastika, a very ancient symbol found all over the Earth, then they heard of the Nazi's misuse of that symbol so it went out of their weaving. We need to realise that all living traditions grow and change along with those who uphold them, and our own old British traditions are no different.

We old ones have kept our ways hidden in plain sight for over two thousand years now; it began when the Romans brought Christianity to our shores. If you didn't agree and practice as Christianity told you to then you are "heretic" and outcast, likely to be tortured and murdered in horrific ways like slow strangulation, which was the old way of hanging before the "long drop" was invented. It really was awful, you hung by your neck from a rope for sometimes as much as twenty or thirty minutes, until you died of a combination of suffocation and strangulation. Or there was the wonderful "catch twenty-two" where you were thrown into a river or pond – if you floated you were a witch and so would be dragged out to be burnt at the stake, if you sank you weren't a witch but you died of drowning anyway. Then, of course, there was being burnt alive at the stake; sometimes on a "slow fire" which meant there was little smoke to suffocate you quickly so you suffered many hours of slow burning. And it wasn't only you and your family who suffered, your familiar spirit, your cat, crow, dog, or toad, or whoever was your friend, would be put into a basket and burned alive in front of your eyes!

I suspect you're getting the idea of why we went into hiding. After two thousand years of practice we're extremely good at it and we didn't come out when all the new age stuff got going, back at the end of the 19th and beginning of the 20th centuries. Some of the most famous new-agers were people like the Russian ex-princess, Helena Blavatsky, an amazing woman who my father's family knew along with her protégé, Annie Bessant, who was the dear friend of my cousin, Esther Bright. From her Russian background, Blavatsky had absorbed a lot of the old ways and was able to get folk interested, less frightened and sceptical, but she didn't know the old ways of Britain and Europe.

Later, in the 1960s, came the academic Mircea Eliade who wrote about his findings from studying "native peoples". Eliade was Romanian born and a professor at the University of Chicago, as well as an historian of religion, fiction writer and philosopher. He opened up the idea of "shamanism" to many people. Later still came Michael Harner. As far as I can discover neither Eliade nor Harner ever came to speak with us old ones in Britain, nor with our fellow-families in Western Europe, both only studied the more obvious shamans that they could see because they look different from "ordinary folk", like the native peoples of the Americas, the Inuit folk, and the Sami. For both Eliade and Harner, we were so well hidden (in plain sight), we didn't exist, and for many people that's still the case now. But we do exist, and we have done for all this time. My people are of the old ones, the old ways are in my bones but you'd never guess if you saw me in the supermarket!

Now, let's get into the numbers ...

Numbers & Patterns

Numbers are amazing, they make wonderful patterns and they work in pairs. Like the DNA double helix, they spiral in and spiral out showing us both evolution and involution ... the patterns of life, and of time.

Figure 2: DNA

In the old ways of Britain, we've used this same idea of the spiral of life since at least the Bronze Age, but we draw it as a labyrinth.

Figure 3: Troytown

We call this labyrinth the Troytown, which is a contraction of the old Welsh-Brythonic name, *Caer y Troieau,* meaning city of coils, or turns, or spirals. Our ancestors had their own ways of understanding the double helix of life.

Spirit & Personality

All the work in this book – and there are exercises to help you understand your own numbers-patterns – runs with this double spiral in mind, the going into the centre and the coming out again. This is how life works; it breathes in and breathes out; it's the cycle of life-death-rebirth, and it works in your numbers too.

The spiral shows us the idea of breathing; you go into the centre and then back out again ... like the breath in your body, you draw the air in, flow it through your heart where you exchange the oxygen it carries for the carbon dioxide your body no longer needs. In work with otherworld you draw in the energy-information otherworld gives you and give back to otherworld, the energy-information you learn from living. The inward spiral takes you into the centre the heart of the goddess, of the Earth; the outward spiral takes you out to the rest of the universe. My childhood experience of being infinitely small (inward spiral) and infinitely huge (outward spiral) is about this too.

We call this involution and evolution. Involution is going deep into the Earth, and into yourself, to *involve* yourself with Earth's plans and help with her needs. Evolution is where you explore and evolve yourself in relation to the rest of the world, the universe and everything, so you become more inclusive and so able to reach out to help others.

So we strive towards something more than our little personal selves, and we learn to be useful to the Earth.

Spirit	Personality
Sun to Earth	Earth to Sun
Widdershins	Deosil

Anticlockwise	Clockwise
Breathing IN	Breathing OUT
Midday to Midnight	Midnight to Midday
Goddess	Guardian God

The spirit-self is the one that lives on through incarnation after incarnation and has good connections with spirit, although we may not know this until we choose to wake up.

The personal-self, like the physical body which contains the spirit for the time of the incarnation, lives only for each lifetime. The personal self is the explorer, adventurer. It goes into its life deeply, learning as much as it can about living and being human. When it dies, it's able to pass on all that learning and experience – through the spirit-self – to its own spirit group in otherworld. That spirit-group then passes the learning on to the whole of otherworld. It's like uploading stuff to "the cloud" in computing so it can be accessed by many people, not just yourself.

The numbers patterns show these two paths, the spirit-self and the personal-self, clearly and help us understand what we're doing here on Earth, this time around. Getting to know these two parts of yourself helps you understand what you're doing here, and what you planned for this incarnation – they really are two sides of one coin – you become whole by knowing and integrating them both.

This integration also helps you to understand death and dying which, perhaps surprisingly, really helps you to live well. You lose the fears, fears of loss, of nihilation, and the fear of losing loved ones too; you come to understand that life and death are two sides of the one coin too, in fact you come to know it in your bones so it's not an intellectual belief but a fact of your life for you. This makes an enormous difference to all your attitudes and your happiness.

Numbers dance the patterns of life and of time. They dance in spirals, inwards and outwards and by so doing they show us the life-journey we planned with our spirit-group before we incarnated this time around. In Britain, we call our spirit-group our *tylwyth*, an old Brythonic word that means people or folk, as in *tylwyth teg* which means fair folk; our tylwyth are our people, our family. They help us plan our life-journey before we even get conceived. Many people lose touch with their tylwyth once they get born or in early childhood, often because the parents begin to supress the "invisible friends" the child talks about; so in order to gain parental approval, the child suppresses the reality they know and begins to learn to live in the small box of the "normal" person. That is not good, and it's the beginning of many hang-ups and problems that plague people all their lives. The parents, with all the best intentions, probably believed they were doing the complete opposite and helping the child to have fewer hang-ups as they grew up. Sigh! We do get things round the backs of our necks too often, don't we?

Understanding your numbers offers you a way out of this maze of "normalcy" and into the labyrinth of living life well.

As in the Troytown labyrinth, our lives are about coming to know ourselves, and know the world in which we live, then we learn how to work with the Earth to help her. The labyrinth leads us into the centre, to know the heart of the matter, the heart of ourselves; then it leads us out again, out into the world so we can learn about what is not-self and integrate that into the wholeness of our being.

Spiral Patterns

So what are these patterns that help you to know so much?

Let's look at how the pairs and the patterns work together in the double spiral. The easiest way to begin this is to play with the old times-tables we learned in our first school.

We'll use the 5 & 4 times-tables as the example so you can begin to see the inward and outward spiralling, the basic pattern that each pair of numbers makes.

5-times table			4-times table			
1x5=5		5	1x4=4			4
2x5=10	1+0=1	1	2x4=8			8
3x5=15	1+5=6	6	3x4=12	1+2=3		3
4x5=20	2+0=2	2	4x4=16	1+6=7		7
5x5=25	2+5=7	7	5x4=20	2+0=2		2
6x5=30	3+0=3	3	6x4=24	2+4=6		6
7x5=35	3+5=8	8	7x4=28	2+8=10	1+0=1	1
8x5=40	4+0=4	4	8x4=32	3+2=5		5
9x5=45	4+5=9	9	9x4=36	3+6=9		9

Figure 4: 5&4 table

Now look ... follow the right-hand column in the 5-times table downwards ... now follow the right-hand column of the 4-times table upwards. Do you see? The numbers of the 5-times and 4-times tables, when reduced to single figures, reverse each other.

The results of the 5-times table numbers go 5 1 6 2 7 3 8 4

The results of the 4-times table numbers go 4 8 3 7 2 6 1 5

They form a pair, their patterns are the same but reversed, like the outward and inward spiral of the Troytown labyrinth, or the DNA double helix, like two sides of one coin ... which is what they are.

The 4-times table holds the personal, half of the spiral where the person explores themselves, self-development, which helps them become properly grownup and inclusive, so they can then work on helping others.

The 5-times table holds the spirit-half of the spiral, it's inclusive, and knows its tylwyth, otherworld, and is able to ask the Earth what she needs and help her plans.

The pair of numbers are two sides of one coin. Each side is vital to the other, the coin would not be whole and complete without both sides. We need to come to know ourselves in context, in relationship with the rest of the cosmos; this is what self-development is about, coming out of the idea that you are the centre of the universe. We then need the inward spiral to help the Earth and our fellow creatures with whom we share our planet. We need to evolve ourselves, so that we can involve ourselves with our Earth.

The journey usually works by us firstly coming to understand our personal selves, and then to grow out of that self-centredness to be able to ask the earth what she needs of us, and then to listen to her, hear her and speak with her, and so be able to be useful to her.

The Earth needs us; she wants us to become her helpers. And we need to do this, to learn and realise that we're not the centre of the universe, that there is so much outside of ourselves that we can connect and work with, learn and know.

This idea of two halves of one coin is beautifully expressed in this ancient brooch from the La Tein era in our British history.

Figure 5: Lady & Lord

Our old British ancestors knew a lot! If you turn one head upside-down you get the other; if you turn the Lady's head upside-down you get the Lord and vice versa. The drawings of the brooch show us that the one *is* the other, and that we cannot have the one without the other. The paired patterns in the numbers show us a similar thing, the outward and inward work of each spiral and what it holds for us.

So all the way through this book we'll be looking at the numbers as pairs, holding duality, being two sides of one coin, for this is how life is, this is how life dances through the patterns of time that the numbers hold. This is how the universe works.

Number Patterns

Now we go on to see the pattern numbers pairs make:

1 with 8
2 with 7
3 with 6
4 with 5

There are 4 different patterns that come out of this – circles, pentagons, triangles and stars. They go like this:

8 & 1 – circles
7 & 2 – pentagons
6 & 3 – triangles
5 & 4 – stars

This 4-ness is another integral part of our old ways. You probably know it better as the elements of earth, water, air and fire but the correlations work across to the number patterns too. To help understand the pairs and the wisdom they hold for you have a look at this table, it gives you a few ideas for correlations …

Figure 6: Element table

Earth	Water	Air	Fire
Winter	Spring	Summer	Autumn
Roots	Leaves	Flowers	Fruit
Body-sensing	Feelings	Thinking	Intuition
8 & 1	7 & 2	6 & 3	5 & 4

The Numbers Circle

To get the picture-patterns the numbers give, you need to use the numbers circle – see diagram. In a moment, you'll see how the number-pairs produce both the inward and outward spirals and how to make the patterns for each number pair.

Draw a circle, like this, and mark it with the numbers as shown – 9 must be at the top.

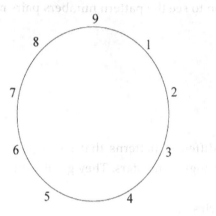

Figure 7: Numbers circle

The other numbers pair with each other on each side of the circle, as shown.

Because no addition of numbers ever comes to zero there's no place for 0 on the numbers circle. Zero has a different function which we'll explore later.

Now we are going to look at the patterns. You'll see each pair makes a pattern specific to itself, and that each member of the pair makes that pattern by going round the circle in the *opposite* way to its partner. This is the fundamental double helix of life again, and the Troytown. Look at these diagrams.

Figure 8: widdershins & deosil spirals

Put your finger on the centre of the left-hand spiral, now follow it to its tail ... your finger has gone round widdershins, anticlockwise. Now do the same for the right-hand spiral ... this time your finger has gone round deosil, clockwise.

These two spirals are like the Lady and the Lord, the two faces of the ancient British brooch. The Lady pulls us *in*, deep within to know ourselves, while the Lord pulls us *out*, out of our little personal selves and to work with the universe. This is duality, how the Lady and the Lord dance, it's how the universe breathes in and out. Is this beginning to make sense?

Circles – 8 & 1

Now you've got some idea of what we're going to do let's actually do it; we'll begin with the 8-times table which pairs with the 1-times table.

8-times table				1-times table	
1x8=8			8	1x1=1	1
2x8=16	1+6=7		7	2x1=2	2
3x8=24	2+4=6		6	3x1=3	3
4x8=32	3+2=5		5	4x1=4	4
5x8=40	4+0=4		4	5x1=5	5
6x8=48	4+8=12	1+2=3	3	6x1=6	6
7x8=56	5+6=11	1+1=2	2	7x1=7	7
8x8=64	6+4=10	1+0=1	1	8x1=8	8
9x8=72	7+2=9		9	9x1=9	9

Figure 9: 8&1 table

Notice again, the reduced numbers of one table are the reverse of the other: the two spirals again, two sides of one coin.

As we reduce each of these two tables we see, again, that the results reverse each other. The 8-times gives us 8,7,6,5,4,3,2,1 and the 1-times gives us 1,2,3,4,5,6,7,8.

Now let's draw the circles.

First let's do the 8-circle. Put your pen on the 8 and draw a line to the 7, from 7 go to 6, from 6 to 5, from 5 to 4, from 4 to 3, from

3 to 2, from 2 to 1, from 1 to 9 and from 9 back home to 8 again.

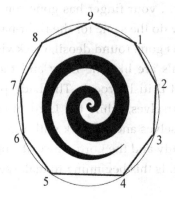

Figure 10: 8 circle

In drawing the 8-circle, you've drawn a circle-like shape going round the numbers and, in doing it, your pen has gone round *widdershins*, anticlockwise, the opposite way round to the sun. This direction, widdershins, draws energy down into the Earth, it's the *inward* spiral, it's about is *turning back* from going home to otherworld to help those still on the path, about returning to Earth to help others and the planet herself too.

Now let's do the circle for the 1-times table. Again, draw the numbers-circle and go round the circle 1, 2, 3, 4, 5, 6, 7, 8, 9, then back to the 1 again.

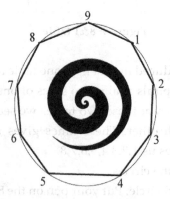

Figure 11: 1 circle

This time your pen went round *deosil*, clockwise, sunwise. This is the *outward* spiral, the personal self, reaches out to find something greater than itself, expands its envelope.

When you've got a handle on yourself, what you want, what drives you and what you're afraid of, then you're able to look beyond yourself, see the bigger picture. But you need to know yourself first in order to do the journey of involution where you do indeed turn back from your own self-development; otherwise you won't really be able let go of your personal needs.

Pentagons – 7 & 2

7-times table				2-times table		
1x7=7			7	1x2=2		2
2x7=14	1+4=5		5	2x2=4		4
3x7=21	2+1=3		3	3x2=6		6
4x7=28	2+8=10	1+0=1	1	4x2=8		8
5x7=35	3+5=8		8	5x2=10	1+0=1	1
6x7=42	4+2=6		6	6x2=12	1+2=3	3
7x7=49	4+9=13	1+3=4	4	7x2=14	1+4=5	5
8x7=56	5+6=11	1=1=2	2	8x2=16	1+6=7	7
9x7=63	6+3=9		9	9x2=18	1+8=9	9

Figure 12: 7&2 table

On the numbers circle, put your pen on the 7, go from 7 to 5, from 5 to 3, from 3 to 1, from 1 to 8, from 8 to 6, from 6 to 4, from 4 to 2, from 2 to 9 and from 9, then back home to 7 again.

Your pen went round widdershins, showing you the 7 times table is another way, the second branch, of the inward spiral drawing you down into the Earth to help those on the path who've not yet walked so far themselves.

And do you see? You've drawn two pentagons ... but there can only be two of them if they share a line. As the numbers 7 and 2 are about love-wisdom and the feeling function, which both include the concept of sharing, this makes sense.

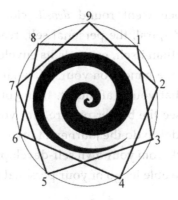

Figure 13: 7 pentagon

Now put your pen on 2, go from 2 to 4, from 4 to 6, from 6 to 8, from 8 to 1, from 1 to 3, from 3 to 5, from 5 to 7, from 7 to 8 and from 9 back home again to 2.

You went round deosil this time, so this is the second branch of the evolutionary spiral and compliments the inward path of the 7.

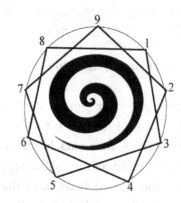

Figure 14: 2 pentagon

Triangles – 6 & 3

6-times table				3-times table		
1x6=6			6	1x3=3		3
2x6=12	1+2=3		3	2x3=6		6
3x6=18	1+8=9		9	3x3=9		9
4x6=24	2+6=6		6	4x3=12	1+2=3	3
5x6=30	3+0=3		3	5x3=15	1+5=6	6
6x6=36	3+6=9		9	6x3=18	1+8=9	9
7x6=42	4+2=6		6	7x3=21	2+1=3	3
8x6=48	4+8=12	1+2=3	3	8x3=24	2+4=6	6
9x6=54	5+4=9		9	9x3=27	2+7=9	9

Figure 15: 6&3 table

Now, put your pen on the 6, move to the 3, then the 9; back to the 6 again, then the 3, then the 9; and, for the third time, go to the 6, then the 3, then back to the 9.

You've done the widdershins circle, making the inward journey again, repeating the triangle three times.

Figure 16: 6 triangle

Now put your pen on the 3, move to the 6, then the 9, and back to the 3 again, then the 6 and the 9; for the third time move the pen to the 3, then the 6, then the 9. Again, you've repeated the pattern three times.

Figure 17: 3 triangle

Spend time pondering this pattern. 3-ness, the triskele, is a strong and fundamental force in the British and many other traditions. It echoes back to the three worlds, and the powers on which our universe is built.

Upperworld	Middleworld	Lowerworld	(3 worlds)
Inspiration	Love	Wisdom	(3 cauldrons)
Smith	Healer	Poet	(3 faces of Brighid)
Maiden	Mother	Crone	(3 faces of the goddess

Figure 18: 3-ness table 1

You'll find these qualities turn up in the numbers, we'll go into it in more depth later.

Stars – 5 & 4

5-times table			4-times table			
1x5=5		5	1x4=4			4
2x5=10	1+0=1	1	2x4=8			8
3x5=15	1+5=6	6	3x4=12	1+2=3		3
4x5=20	2+0=2	2	4x4=16	1+6=7		7
5x5=25	2+5=7	7	5x4=20	2+0=2		2
6x5=30	3+0=3	3	6x4=24	2+4=6		6
7x5=35	3+5=8	8	7x4=28	2+8=10	1+0=1	1
8x5=40	4+0=4	4	8x4=32	3+2=5		5
9x5=45	4+5=9	9	9x4=36	3+6=9		9

Figure 19: 5&4 tables

Put your pen on the 5 and round you go, widdershins, from 5 to
1, 1 to 6, 6 to 2, 2 to 7, 7 to 3, 3 to 8, 8 to 4, 4 to 9 and 9 back home
to 5 again. This makes a beautiful nine-pointed star.

Figure 20: 5 star

Now put your pen on the 4 and go round deosil, sun-wise from
4 to 8, 8 to 3, 3 to 7, 7 to 2, 2 to 6, 6 to 1, 1 to 5, 5 to 9 and from
9 back home to 4, again making another 9-pointed star in the
opposite direction.

Figure 21: 4 star

Starting on the left-hand row numbers you can start to make a pattern. Start on the left-hand side you can start to make a beautiful picture, a 4 star.

Now put your pen on the 9 and you could draw a curve from 9 to 4, then 2 to 5, then 7 to 3, then 6 to 1. You can also name it 5, again, making another beautiful picture, the opposite direction.

8 & 1 – Infinity and the Personal Self

8-times table				1-times table	
1x8=8			8	1x1=1	1
2x8=16	1+6=7		7	2x1=2	2
3x8=24	2+4=6		6	3x1=3	3
4x8=32	3+2=5		5	4x1=4	4
5x8=40	4+0=4		4	5x1=5	5
6x8=48	4+8=12	1+2=3	3	6x1=6	6
7x8=56	5+6=11	1+1=2	2	7x1=7	7
8x8=64	6+4=10	1+0=1	1	8x1=8	8
9x8=72	7+2=9		9	9x1=9	9

Figure 22: 8&1 tables

8	1
Circle	Circle
Infinity	Ridgepole
Integrated self	Personal self
Spirit	Matter

8 pairs with 1. 8 is all curves while 1 is a straight line; they are opposites for good reason. Both 8 and 1 work with forces which generate life.

8-ness: Infinity

The number 8, on its side, is also the symbol for infinity

Figure 23: Infinity

First of all, get paper and pen and spend some time drawing 8s, get the feel into your hand, arm and body. 8, like all the numbers, is more than an intellectual exercise.

As you draw the 8s your pen flows round one circle, crosses over and flows round the other. If you're right-handed you probably began your first circle going widdershins, got half way through it and turned deosil to do the bottom circle. You then crossed back over and went widdershins again to complete the top one. Left-handed people often do it the other way around.

Keep going round and round, over your 8, keep doing it. You find yourself travelling first one way and then the other. The figure 8 is one of the simplest spiral labyrinths, it goes in both directions, deosil, widdershins, deosil, widdershins. Remember, deosil is clockwise and widdershins is anticlockwise. This property of 8-ness is like the labyrinth again, fundamental to how it works with spirit, it brings together the two directions, widdershins and deosil, the energies of feminine and masculine, the pairs of opposites.

Now try drawing 8 on its side as the infinity symbol above, a similar but different feel.

So what is Infinity? Hmmm! Difficult! Eternity, immensity, endless, boundless, limitless, perpetuity, time without end. Like I said, difficult to imagine, at least at first.

Nowadays, we're educated and encouraged to think of things as having a beginning and an end. While this may be convenient and comfortable, it has little to do with reality, or physics! You've likely heard of the Big Bang Theory which suggests a beginning for the universe and is much quoted on TV but ... but ... if you talk to scientists, the real ones who're at the cutting edge of theoretical and particle physics, you'll find them talking about the fact that the maths for the Big Bang don't really hold up. And, anyway, what was there before the Big Bang, what did it come out of and what set it off? So the world, the universe and everything (nor any unified theory of everything either!) is not a comfy beginning-middle-end story, like a soap on TV, it's a deep, confusing, difficult concept that nobody has got the hang of yet.

And yet we live in it and with it all the time, we're constantly part of infinity. We are infinitely part of infinity.

Einstein showed that matter can neither be created nor destroyed. It changes constantly. And it completely confuses us because current photographs of the universe seem to show us that it's constantly expanding. How? If matter is not created then how is the universe expanding? I'm not going further with this in this book, but it does strongly suggest to me the concept of a "breathing" universe. I find all that stuff fascinating; comes of having a mathematician-physicist-husband, who's talked all this stuff to me over the cornflakes for the past forty-five years.

Wow! Breathing universes and the Big Bang – that's a huge load of stuff to take on if you happen to be an 8-person and so have connections with infinity. We can make it a bit smaller than that though, and so a bit easier to get a handle on. There's an old song from Yorkshire which does it rather well … *On Ilkley Moor Baht'at* … these are the words, in the dialect:

Wheear 'as ta bin sin ah saw thee,
On Ilkla Moor baht 'at?!
Wheear 'as ta bin sin ah saw thee?
On Ilkla Moor baht 'at

Tha's been a cooartin' Mary Jane
On Ilkla Moor baht 'at
Tha's been a cooartin' Mary Jane
On Ilkla Moor baht 'at

Tha's bahn t'catch thi deeath o'cowd
On Ilkla Moor baht 'at
Tha's bahn t'catch thi deeath o'cowd
On Ilkla Moor baht 'at

Then we shall ha' to bury thee

On Ilkla Moor baht 'at
Then we shall ha' to bury thee
On Ilkla Moor baht 'at

Then t'worms 'll cum and eat thee oop
On Ilkla Moor baht 'at
Then t'worms 'll cum and eat thee oop
On Ilkla Moor baht 'at

Then ducks 'll cum and eat oop t'worms
On Ilkla Moor baht 'at
Then ducks 'll cum and eat oop t'worms
On Ilkla Moor baht 'at

Then we shall go an' ate oop ducks
On Ilkla Moor baht 'at
Then we shall go an' ate oop ducks
On Ilkla Moor baht 'at

Then we shall all 'ave etten thee
On Ilkla Moor baht 'at
Then we shall all 'ave etten thee
On Ilkla Moor baht 'at

That's wheer we get us oahn back
On Ilkla Moor baht 'at
That's wheer we get us oahn back
On Ilkla Moor baht 'at

So the poor lassie catches her death of cold, dies and is buried; the worms eat her up; the ducks eat the worms; we eat the ducks … and so we eat her atoms, or rather the atoms that made up her body while she was alive. We don't eat her spirit, of course. And that happens all through everyone's, and everything's, life

– you eat, digest, excrete, and your excretions become part of the next meal for someone or something. In the sense of our physical atoms, we are all part of each other and always have been.

This works even if you go back before the Earth was solid, before all the atoms stuck themselves together to make this glorious spinning ball of rock we all live on. The atoms came from stardust (as Joni Mitchell wrote) – *We are stardust, we are golden, we are billion-year-old carbon, And we got to get ourselves back to the garden.* Only it's one hell of a lot older than the mere billion years that she wrote about, our own earth is at least 4.5 billion years old for a start, and then there's however-long that the atoms were cycling around the universe before they came together as the Earth, and nobody has the answer to that one. I'll let Joni off though as the lines do scan well!

Infinity is about this constant change, the constant reusing and recycling of atoms from one being to another ... and so is all life. And so is 8-ness. It's about beginning to allow glimmers of this reality into your consciousness, about expanding your personal envelope to encompass more. There's no way anyone manages this all in one go, nor should you try to, after all infinity is endlessness, there is no need for an end; it's about the continuous growth of your consciousness, and your ability to be inclusive, your ability to relate to everything and to know, ken, your interconnection with all life.

8 also gives us the linking threads to the ancestral realm which includes everything, not just our grannies; it also links us to the world of potential, connecting us with the unlimited, latent, dormant and embryonic inspiration of ideas and concepts. The world of the ancestors has great wisdom for us, and advice on how *not* to do things; how not to re-make the mistakes of the past, as well as idea for doing things we've not yet thought of.

Being an 8-person
8 is on the *centripetal* inward cycle. Centripetal is about being

drawn into the centre, the axis. It's a force which acts on a body moving in a circular path around a centre, which pulls that body inwards, towards the centre around which it's moving. Spirit is about this centripetal force, about 'inspiriting matter', bringing heaven down to earth.

Like with all numbers, there are extremes which cause the person to go out of harmony, out of right relation with the world in which they live. To work well with your numbers you have to balance yourself between these extremes, like walking a tightrope, it's often called 'the razor-edged path' in esoteric-speak. When you're balanced it's like standing at that centre where the two circles of the 8 meet.

It's very easy, as you may have found in your drawing, to get hypnotised into just flowing round and round the spiral. You don't want to stop, it feels so good. Now, take this idea into life … it can be a 'go with the flow', but if you take it to extremes you flow so much you lose all identity, all individuation, you become without direction, and you lose the ability to concentrate and focus. This is no good at all for your spirit. Your spirit-self has real difficulty inhabiting a gossamer-cobweb person who wafts hither and yon, going with the flow; there's no security, no grail-cauldron to contain it, or for it to express itself through, there's no vehicle in which to do its work. It's like grabbing at clouds.

So 8-people have to take care that, while they do go with the flow, they *also* have edges and boundaries, they know self from not-self, and are distinct enough not to invade other people's space. They have to be able, over their lifetime, to form their personal self into a solid and useful grail-cup in which their spirit can live and work. This is, after all, part of the bargain they made before they came into incarnation this time.

At the other end of the scale 8-people can become rigid. They walk their spiral, but they tread so religiously in their own footsteps that eventually they find themselves treading a deep, narrow rut, always the same, no change, no growth, no evolution. Deep ruts are very hard and difficult to climb out of. Imagine to yourself how it feels to be walking in a track, just the width of your footsteps, and perhaps so deep you can no longer see over the top. How do you climb out? And your view of the rest of the world would be severely limited, comprising largely of a strip of sky and perhaps the feet and ankles of other people who come close to the edge of your rut. You've probably got the picture ... now ponder and explore those analogies in terms of everyday life and relationships.

A simple example might be the way you drive or walk to work. Maybe you always take the same route. This can be very comforting and reassuring, you can listen to the radio, you don't have to think, and you go on autopilot ... Now ... is this *always* a good thing? Maybe you need a change, to see something different, feel your brain firing at full capacity again and enjoying it. While routine is good and useful and pleasant it can also become a treadmill which excludes growth. Our spirits won't thank us for that. And we become dull and boring companions for our friends and loved ones too – not surprising if they forget our birthday, or up and leave, perhaps!

1-ness: the Personal Self

1 is the partner of 8.

Again, get paper and pen and draw the 1 as a straight line. Leave off the little flip at the top, keep it as straight line, this way you'll get the feeling of 'line', as you did with the floating curve of 8.

Let the feeling flow into your body through your hand and arm. Don't try to translate the feeling, just experience it for the moment. Later, having put all feel of 1-ness into your Cauldron of the Unconscious, when it's brewed awhile you'll be able to eat of the idea-soup it contains. Like all cooking, you have to let it brew and remember, a watched pot never boils, so leave it alone to work away without you fussing over it. The Cauldron of the Unconscious works this way, so let it happen, don't try to understand or explain it to yourself (and definitely not to anyone else). Give it time to develop into a juicy, nourishing broth, then you can really feast on it.

The number 1 is on the centrifugal function, the outward spiral, it's expansive and inclusive, it's that feeling like spinning a ball round on a string, the ball feels as though it's pulling away from you. Or if you're driving a car fast round a corner you feel as if you're being pulled/pushed away sideways from the apex of the corner.

As you've already seen, each of the pairs of numbers adds to 9, the number of the Void, of potential, of enabling power – we talk about this in detail later. Because of this pairing, as an 8-person you also need to work with the 1, and if you are a 1-person you need to work with the 8, to understand your full nature.

The other half of your number pair will be your shadow side – and shadows are vital in order to show you the edges that define you from everything else. Shadow enables you to see! Shadow shows you the boundary between you and not-you, it makes you visible as you. Shadow is what makes it possible to define, to know where you are. You need your shadow or you could end up like Peter Pan.

The Ridgepole & the Personal Self

1 is the Ridgepole. In Taoist philosophy it's the ridgepole that holds up heaven, by standing firm on the earth. The number 1 keeps heaven and earth distinct and separate – it's both an edge and a boundary. It defines the pairs of opposites and so makes our universe possible.

So 1 has a very important *divisive* function that is good and necessary. In some new-age work we may be told divisiveness is 'wrong' but this is a somewhat simplistic notion as it leaves out all the important material about boundaries, edges, self/not-self, individuation, and duality without which our universe cannot properly function, and nor can we. 1 is a number of discernment, knowing one thing from another, and without this faculty we wouldn't be able to know our arse from our elbow as the ancient and slightly rude adage goes. It's about Jung's *sensory* function, about the body, about the stuff of matter, and the relation of our body with earth.

Knowing *self* from *other* is vital and necessary, essential to knowing. Without knowing we become 'head-sets', full of knowledge which we splurge out inappropriately, swamping our hearers and blinding them with science. The number 1 brings us back to our bodies, back to earth, feet on the ground. Part of knowing is knowing when to speak and when to be silent, how much/little to say, and that's a hallmark of the fully awake and aware 1-person. It does take a bit of practice and making a few mistakes to get to this point but that's OK, it's very likely the sun will continue to rise each morning in spite of our mistakes, a comforting thought. But it's not a reason for being thoughtless and hedonistic, which are downside traits for 1-people; so while making mistakes is OK and useful, galumphing about without caring or thinking is not.

When you were drawing 1s you will have felt the up-down, rocking, pendulum motion of the figure. It's a journey between two points. Polarities. If you draw up and down over the same line it's quite hypnotic, probably boring, and makes a hole in the paper. Think about that.

Being a 1-person

If you are a 1-person it's very possible to get stuck, to lose perspective, get tunnel vision. All you can see is those two points, and the only journey you can imagine is the one that goes between them. A 1-person who has got into this state can be quite aggressive to anyone who suggests there might be another way. The 8 has its 'stuck in a groove', and so does the 1, but this stuck-ness feels very different for each of them although, to an outside observer, their 'stuck-ness' is both obvious and similar.

1-people, because of their strong heaven/earth polarity, can be quite difficult to coax out of their rut. Helpers must learn to duck fast as 1-people can lash out like lightning, so fancy footwork is a good idea for those who would like to help, and 1-people are very worthwhile helping. They are towers of strength; the figure 1 is a tower-like image, and 1-people can be swords to fight battles, often for others than themselves and for causes which they espouse. Where these causes are evolutionary – such as the environment, education, stopping cruelty, greed and poverty, for instance – the 1-person can be an exceptional leader. Leadership is a fundamental trait of 1-ness, up-front and out there; 1-people do this very well, they can also stimulate change and stand as marker-posts at crossroads. What they, and the world, need of them is for them to have a good handle on discrimination *before* they rush to sort the world out.

1-ness is also about beginnings. 1-people initiate things. They also have to learn to complete them, a function of the line which *goes all the way* between two points.

So the basic extremes for 1-people are stuck-ness, getting in a rut, narrow vision and pushing everyone else along with their idea of right. These are qualities of a self-image which has become distorted through introspection, as they are also excellent naval-gazers. The 1-person can become so singular that, to quote an excellent Harrison Ford film, they feel that *'Everyone's lost but me!'* With loving help 1-people can be persuaded to climb out of this pit.

Another word for 1-people can be *poised* like the grace and balance of a tight-rope walker; there's a lovely Arthur Rackham picture of fairies dancing along a strand of cobweb which gives a sense of this.

7 & 2 – Love/Wisdom and the Feeling Self

7-times table				2-times table		
1x7=7			7	1x2=2		2
2x7=14	1+4=5		5	2x2=4		4
3x7=21	2+1=3		3	3x2=6		6
4x7=28	2+8=10	1+0=1	1	4x2=8		8
5x7=35	3+5=8		8	5x2=10	1+0=1	1
6x7=42	4+2=6		6	6x2=12	1+2=3	3
7x7=49	4+9=13	1+3=4	4	7x2=14	1+4=5	5
8x7=56	5+6=11	1=1=2	2	8x2=16	1+6=7	7
9x7=63	6+3=9		9	9x2=18	1+8=9	9

Figure 24: 7&2 tables

7	2
Pentagon	Pentagon
Love/Wisdom	Desire
Inclusion	Separation
Flowing	Water

7-ness: Love/Wisdom

As before, begin getting to know 7-ness by drawing 7s. You begin with a line going horizontally from left to right, then you dive down on a diagonal from right to left. Now your pen comes off the paper, then back down onto it again to draw a horizontal line across the downward diagonal. NB – for this exercise, *cross your sevens*, like in the picture, even if you don't normally do this, you'll see why when you come to explore 2.

Figure 25: 7 crossed

Drawing 7 has a rhythm, doesn't it? Da-da-dum, a bit like a waltz.

7 is about Love/Wisdom. What is this? Love is part of everything in life. It's easy to love foolishly and we all do it, it's a much more delicate process to love wisely. It's also very easy to be wise after the event, we all have 20/20 hindsight. Again, it requires a lot of intelligent (not clever!) care and thought in order to be wise lovingly, or to be lovingly wise. When we have this little conundrum under our belts we are much more acceptable human beings than we were before.

What is it, to love? Poets, essayists, novelists, film-makers, psychotherapists, singers, Uncle-Tom-Cobley-and-All have gone on about love for millennia. Lovers tend to get on with enjoying it and/or messing it up for themselves, and everyone around them. Most of us *know* love when we see it or feel it, but how to say what it is?

Exercise: Love

When you feel love for a person, an animal, a place or whatever, what happens? What sensations come over you? Ponder on this now, just sit with the idea. Call to mind someone or somewhere you love dearly and allow yourself to experience the sensations which come as you do this. Don't try to control or analyse them, and certainly don't censor them. Jot down brief word-pointers to remind you of the sensations after the exercise.

You may well find yourself 'going off', not seeing the everyday world but watching the person or place with your *mind's eye*. Allow this to happen. Come back to normality very gently as the experience wanes.

When you're ready, write some words in answer to the following questions. Don't try to make sense, be grammatical, spell correctly or write neatly, let go of all that and just put down the first words which come into your head.

How did your body feel as you began?

What sensations ran through your body as you brought the person/place to mind?

Did your body shake? Tears, smile, other movement?

Were you sexually aroused?

Did you have sensations so intense as to be called exquisite?

What sensations came as the image began to fade? [you might feel *both* loss and relief at the same time – that's OK]

How did your body feel after the experience was ended?

When you have jotted down responses to the stimuli-questions put your paper down, go and make yourself a hot drink. Take your drink along with your piece of paper and go somewhere else, *don't* go back to the same physical environment in which you had the experience. Make sure it's somewhere you can curl up comfortably for a whole half-hour on your own. Talking will wreck the whole experience, so don't, however tempted you may be to splash your nearest and dearest with the marvellous revelations which have just come to you. Hold them secret, and sacred, for a while.

You have just had an experience of Love. *And* you've also found your own words to remind yourself of how it was. You've not had to take on my words (or anyone else's) which, while they fit me like a glove, are all the wrong shape and size for you. By the way, if nothing happened you just picked the wrong person or place. Try another.

Pain may well have been one of the ingredients of your experience and this may surprise you. Pain is a part of love, without any need for sadism or masochism. Things can be so exquisitely beautiful they hurt. A painful time, perhaps a death or loss, can also be incredibly beautiful and full of joy ... but it still hurts. If there is no pain then there is no real love, only emotional attachment and desire, and these are 2-qualities not 7-ness. The pain of love is not that of a thwarted child but of an adult who is seeing and feeling far beyond themselves. This is what love is about.

The pattern for 7 and 2 is two pentagons ... but remember ... they can each only be pentagrams by *sharing* a line. If one pentagram takes all five lines to itself then the other is incomplete. Do you see the analogy here? Love cannot be alone, it is always about sharing. Each side of the love-partnership responds, gives back to us. We share a common thread with our love, as the pentagons share a common line, it is this willing sharing that enables love to be whole.

Being a 7-person

7 is the inward, centripetal, and downward spiral from heaven to earth, the in-breathing. It's about intimate personal love, *and* about the expansive love for all creation, both at once. It's also about the wisdom which knows how to love in each unique individual situation. 7-ness is very much a feeling of "this and that", the and/and principle.

One of the downside tendencies of 7-ness can be a propensity to drift off, to disappear into that glorious world of loving you just experienced and refuse to come back. A wish for the *beauty* of without the *work* which enables it, 7 is the *inward* half of this pair. A number's down-side is often the up-side of its partner. In this context it's worth recalling the words of an old master, *"Evil is inappropriate good"*, ponder on that ... just how much "inappropriate good" have you done in your life? Ouch!

So 7-people can wish to be gone from this world which they may see as a vale of tears. Those who trap themselves in fairyland this way often find it impossible to love in the real world. They may tell themselves, and everyone else, that this is right and proper and as it should be; that they are meant to love higher things. But, in fact, they've become so heavenly they're no earthly use!

Another downside trait can be to become addicted to these wonderful feelings and use anyone and everyone to get more of them.

Then there's the very subtle down-side of when the 7-person who "gives everything away". At first glance, and certainly to themselves, this can seem like the ultimate act, the ultimate gift, the giving away of everything we have. However, a closer look shows it to be more like "spiritual anorexia", or sometimes bulimia. Both physical conditions often root in a person's feelings of unworthiness, feeling undeserving. There are often similar roots for the spiritual conditions; some people feel spiritually unworthy, no good, useless, see everyone around them apparently far more "advanced" than themselves. This can make them either starve themselves of spirit, because they're unworthy, or binge-eat of lots of different courses and workshops only to sick up all they got from them, and then begin all over again. this is bad for both your personal-self and your spirit-self, just as the physical effects of anorexia and bulimia are for your physical body.

Another downside of 7-people is the need to be loved which can come out as approval seeking which means the 7-person can be coerced into behaviour which is against their nature. It's a hard trait to get out of because it requires the person to risk losing the love they think/believe they have in order to become themselves, which can seem to be a fate worse than death.

Sometimes wise love requires us to stand back and allow disaster to happen so that learning can ensue. That requires we put sentimentalism and some of what might be called "motherliness and caring" out the window. It can appear cold and unfeeling to feeling-based people who are not yet come to wisdom, so it's a difficult and often misunderstood balance-point and, in consequence, can be hard to maintain.

The balanced Love/Wisdom person can be an excellent consciousness teacher. They learn from everyone and everything they meet ... books, TV, films, friends in the pub, whatever, it all goes into the cauldron, along with the germ of a new idea, and brews until it becomes a part of themselves. Then they are able to offer it to people and be heard. They are enchanters in the old sense; to en-chant is the practice of using voice and words to enfold the listeners in new thinking, new seeing, new knowing. The enchanter who uses this wisely to enable others is a consciousness teacher. They will be one who has learned the deep meaning of language and the deep workings of the Earth and the elements, so they're able to bring them all together and portray the wholeness which they perceive, in a manner that others can grasp. This is quite a feat and although it's within the possibility of all of us, 7 people have (if they choose) a bit of a head start.

Of course, this ability to enchant can also be used to obtain and maintain power over others, and that is something the 7-person must always be aware of. We can all think of historical examples of people who've had this power.

2-ness: The Feelings Self

2 is the partner of 7. As before, draw the figure 2 lots of times. See how similar the body-movements are to those you made when drawing the crossed 7. You begin with a line going from left to right, from the unconscious to the conscious; then your pen goes down on the diagonal from right to left, from the conscious to the unconscious; finally, you make a horizontal line going from left to right again, from the unconscious to the conscious again. These are the same movements that you made when you drew the crossed 7, *except* that your pen came off the paper to cross the 7, and it stays on the paper to make the bottom stroke of the 2.

These three moves of your pen, from unconscious to conscious, then conscious to unconscious and finally unconscious to conscious again are significant. There's an old Zen adage which goes like this ...

In the beginning the trees are trees and the mountains are mountains.
Then the trees are no longer trees and the mountains no longer mountains.
Then the trees are trees again, and the mountains are mountains.

A riddle indeed, but is it beginning to filter its way into your bones? Allow it time and space now, perhaps over a cup of tea, allow it to move into your consciousness.

The adage describes the process of the three pen-strokes as we pass through the different aspects of the unconscious and the conscious. It is, strangely and paradoxically, possible to be consciously unconscious, however it takes a while to achieve this so don't be in a rush. Glimmers of illumination sneak up on us if we just put the notion into our cauldron and allow it to brew there until it (not we!) is ready to be seen.

2 brings the centrifugal, the *outward* urge towards something greater than self which helps us begin to change and grow so we become inclusive enough to be the home for our spirit self.

2 is about in the sense of I-and-thou, polarity and duality again, both sides of the coin, and the pairs of opposites. In 1-ness we explored this as the line which travels between two points, separation and individuation. Now, in 2-ness, we explore a different facet, we see things as part of a whole *as well as* individual things in their own right.

2 is about the aspect of our personal self to do with Jung's feeling-function. It is the weaving between polarities, like the movement to draw both the figures 2 and 7, and it's this *movement between* the polarities that enables feelings to happen and be expressed. Without the polarities there would be no

feelings, we would be stuck, static, stationary with nowhere to move, nowhere to go. It is *movement* which is the medium. Feelings are the e-motions which move us, desire is the power-house for change and growth, the spurs and lures which tease us out of our status quo. They get us to step out of our front door which, as Bilbo says, is a very dangerous thing, because we set our foot on the road and, unless we keep our feet, we can be swept off goodness knows where. We probably will be anyway because we need to expand our envelope, to *"boldly go where no-one has gone before"* if we're going to grow.

Exercise: Good & Bad Points

Get a piece of paper – do it on paper, not on your computer! – and write down all your good points on one side of a page and all your bad points on the other. Which list is longer?

Now, leave the piece of paper around (with a pen) where you can add to it over the next few days. Make a point of discovering more of the nice bits of you and writing them down. Grow that good-side list. Loveable people tend to be a balanced mix of good and bad. And they're comfortable with their bad bits, they don't over-stress them by rejecting and trying to get rid of them. Neither works. What does work is to accept them without any great emphasis, and to befriend them. One of my teachers used to tell me to take my bad bits and sit down together with them with a cup of coffee and a delicious Polish doughnut. *"After a little bit of enjoying yourselves,"* she would say, *"your horrid bits will come back to normal size."* And she was right. Often, I'd been making mountains out of molehills and so felt quite inadequate to change ... don't we all?

This is important. It's too easy, and we're often encouraged by our peers and those we look up to, to concentrate on our bad bits and to try to "improve" – which almost always means become like the other person thinks we ought to be. We try to live normal-scripts, to fit into boxes, we cut bits of our toes and heels off in order to fit our feet into someone else's glass slipper. Bad! So work on that good-column as well as the bad one. And ... take the bad one to somewhere comfy, with your favourite coffee/tea and piece of cake or Polish doughnut, and sit with the bad bits, watch them come back to their proper size.

Being a 2-person

The feeling function is very strong in all of us, even if we apparently suppress it; indeed, if you think about it, this suppression is also an *expression* of feelings we don't want to show. Nowadays people do know a little about being emotionally-literate, i.e. being able to have feelings and express them without being embarrassed by them, and also without causing damage to others or themselves by having them.

Being led and ruled by their feelings is the paramount extreme for 2-people, so they may have some trouble getting their emotionally literacy right.

2-people can believe it is the emotions, the feelings, which hold the spirit but this isn't the case. Spirit is above both love-wisdom and desire. However, there are many similarities between desire and love-wisdom which require work and pondering to determine, so the 2-person becomes able see the difference between them.

2-people can have a strong tendency to follow the lead of their feelings and allow their emotions to rule their lives and this can be a subtle thing, especially now we are much encouraged to "express our feelings" in the current world. Whilst it is good to express feeling you do need to have done the discernment between expressing them and being ruled by them, and be able to do this without kidding yourself. Extreme examples of out-of-control expression of feelings are when people take everything personally, are grossly sympathetic, unable to sit back and allow someone to go through pain, but want to "make everything better".

Taking everything personally is a common down-side of 2-ness and a root of the rages which stem from it. To take everything personally subtly inflates the ego until, usually without realising it, we become the centre of the world ... to ourselves. Anything which hurts us *must* have been directed to do so, the person intended our hurt. In reality, the person who bumped into us in the supermarket queue probably didn't even notice us, and there's another subconscious grievance ... they didn't even see us! This is a fear which lurks in back of the unconscious for the feelings-inflated 2-person, "Perhaps I'm *not* the centre of the universe. Perhaps I'm so insignificant nobody notices me!" That can be a very hard one to bring to the surface. 2-people need to find a way of expressing their feelings which also helps them accept their own responsibility for those feelings.

2-people share with 7-people the approval-seeking urge and the need to be loved. They usually come at it more aggressively than 7-people but the roots are similar. Both feel insecure in their personalities and so reach outwards for love rather than inwards. To be loved means you are loveable ... but to be loveable you must love yourself.

2-people are often very good at knocking themselves down but lousy at appreciating their good points – back to that good-points bad-points exercise. This can easily make them dull, boring and aggressive ... and consequently not very loveable. Both 2 and 7 people benefit from time alone, time to make friends with themselves, so they come to accept both their warts and their good points. As you likely found in the exercise, it can often be those good points which are hardest to accept, a far worse stumbling block than the warts.

Remember those pictures of balance? Being a 2-person is another case where the normal idea of balance – two equal weights either side of the fulcrum – doesn't usually work out. It's very easy to get stuck in that idea and not realise that equal weights imply stuckness, and hard to move out of that "equal" position because it's not dynamic. Back to walking again, in order to take that first step, you have to move your balance from both feet to one foot, otherwise you can't lift the other foot off the ground to step forward! Try that again now, get up now and walk across the room ... how was that? To move forward (or backward, or sideways) you had to go off rigid balance and put yourself into a dynamic, off-centre balance. It may feel risky now you think about it – ponder on that, translate it into your everyday life situations.

6 & 3 – Knowing and Thinking/Reasoning

6-times table				3-times table		
1x6=6			6	1x3=3		3
2x6=12	1+2=3		3	2x3=6		6
3x6=18	1+8=9		9	3x3=9		9
4x6=24	2+6=6		6	4x3=12	1+2=3	3
5x6=30	3+0=3		3	5x3=15	1+5=6	6
6x6=36	3+6=9		9	6x3=18	1+8=9	9
7x6=42	4+2=6		6	7x3=21	2+1=3	3
8x6=48	4+8=12	1+2=3	3	8x3=24	2+4=6	6
9x6=54	5+4=9		9	9x3=27	2+7=9	9

Figure 26: 6&3 tables

6-ness: Knowing

Begin by drawing the figure 6. Feel that rhythm as your pen slides from the top right, round in a curve to the bottom where it curls round then reverses upwards to join itself at the middle. 6, 6, 6, 6, you make a half-moon, anti-clockwise then curve back on yourself to make a full circle, full moon, at the bottom.

6 is about *knowing*, kenning, remember? Remember the bucket of water analogy I gave earlier? It's the ability to know something without reasoning it or necessarily being able to put it into words. It's the quality which overlights the thinking function which is about intellect and reasoning, the thinking function belongs to the 3-half of this pair.

6 is about bringing ideas into matter and is sometimes called Active Intelligence in esoteric-speak, it's what enables the images and visions of spirit to be seen and later made real in this world. Without knowing, kenning, we cannot properly appreciate this inspiration. And we need the other half of this pair, 3-ness, to structure and shape them into forms. Without forms, the ideas and visions would waft about like lost ghosts, and many do just that because there is no 3-ness function to give them a skeleton

on which their form can be woven by the knowing, kenning of 6-ness.

Being a 6-person?

Wise owl is a good image and also holds some of the extreme-position difficulties common to 6-people. Owls are brilliant twilight and night hunters, they have fantastic night-vision and wonderfully precise hearing; they can pinpoint a mouse on the barn floor below by sound alone and then stoop straight onto it, and their wings are made so that they fly silently. Owls often mate for life too, although they may go off on their own, for a holiday, after mating and bringing up their young, returning together again in the autumn and early winter to re-establish their bond.

Owls have been symbols of wisdom in many traditions for millennia and many goddesses, such as Blodeuwedd, have them as their totem-beast. Florence Nightingale, a real force for change in the world and in nursing, had a little Scops Owl, called Athena, who she rescued in Athens and hand reared so the bird became her constant companion, travelling everywhere and nesting in her pocket.

Most owls are not very awake and aware during daylight, the Little Owl is an exception as it regularly flies during the day and may be seen sat on posts, watching and hunting. But most owls are not geared up for bright light and may become dazzled and confused by it. If Tawny Owls emerge during the day they are often mobbed by other birds, even the little ones like sparrows, wrens and tits, who flock together and dive-bomb the poor owl until it goes back into hiding in its tree-hole.

It can be like this with 6-people. Knowing, seeing the meaning in things, is not always acceptable in the bright light of everydayness because such knowing tends to upturn established and comfortable apple-carts, and that's not to most people's tastes. The knowers, 6-people, need to learn to know when their knowing is going to be well received and when to keep their beaks shut. They also need to learn not to stuff their knowing down everyone's throat, unasked for. There's yet another old adage, now a motto of the Special Air Services (SAS) in Britain, *"To know, to dare, to be silent,"* which is well worth 6-people taking on board. The daring is often about that subtle form of risk, daring *not* to speak, which can be much harder to take and do than the risk of speaking. It's about daring to be silent, which means allowing people and things to take their own course, despite any knowing you might have of outcomes, learning to button up and not shoot your mouth off.

Additionally, knowing 6-people can also have so much wisdom and information flowing through them that they'll talk the hind-legs off whole beachfuls of donkeys. This tends to put their audience off. They have to learn when to act and when to refrain from action. And 6-people can so lose touch with their 3-half, their shadow self, that they fail to put a good structure on the information and the knowing they wish to impart, as a consequence, their audience may feel as if they've been scatter-blasted with Jello! Not constructive.

The wise owl can also be the absent-minded professor. Knowing can be filed in the Heap-System. Yes, the owl may know just where everything is and they will undoubtedly affirm that they do, usually spluttering in their beaks all the while. But, when it comes right down to it, they may need to investigate several heaps before happening on the right one.

There can also be a squirrel tendency, hoarding tons of dusty information, carting dozens of mouldy bags around, none of which has been used for aeons. Another thing squirrels do is to bury nuts all over the place forget where they buried them. For trees, this is really useful as it gets their seeds proliferated all over the place and builds new woodland as the forgotten nuts germinate and grow. It doesn't work quite so well for 6-people, they often end up with the equivalent of gardens full of the wrong sorts of trees, all crowded together so they don't grow properly and cut out all the light. The 6-person needs to take a machete to the lot in order to get some life back in the mental forest.

The awake and aware 6-person is able to grow a magical, enchanted forest, full of sunlit groves and dark glades, a marvellous habitat for magical and spirit wildlife. This forest will have the right layering of tall, ancient trees, a mid-layer of faster growing and shorter-lived trees, and the bushes and plants of the bottom layer. Think about that habitat inside yourself, this is how to become your own perfect spirit ecosystem.

Balanced 6-people work with the magical mental energy that enables us to know, ken, things. It is the kenning that helps us to feel a part of everything, to know it in our bones, and which takes away the lonely feelings of separation that come of not being sure, not being certain, that we really are part of a whole. This knowing is about the connective energy-threads which everything (not just human beings) sends out so that it can be connected to everything else. This is like the mycorrhiza who carry the water and food all across the land and play important roles in soil biology and soil chemistry.

As an analogy, plants grown in nutrient-deficient, sterile soils and growth media perform poorly without the addition of spores of mycorrhizal fungi to colonise the plant roots and aid in the uptake of soil mineral nutrients. The absence of mycorrhizal fungi will slow and even stop plant growth on degraded landscapes such as those ravaged by modern industrial farming. It seems, from preserved fossil plants, that mycorrhizal networks been around for at least 400 million years, but ploughing breaks and cuts them so the linkages across the land, across the whole Earth, are destroyed. Plants don't cope with this, and there's a big knock-on effect for animals (and us human animals) too.

The mycorrhiza of spirit work similarly. One of the things the 6-person can do is assist all those around them to build up their spirit-mycorrhiza, their connecting threads which we call "deer trods" here in Britain. This way, we rebuild our interconnectedness with all things and will find ways to help the Earth repair herself too.

It's part of learning to walk the path, walk the deer trods, and become a walker between worlds. We discover our own threads and their connections to everything else, at a deeper level of knowing, and this shows us how we are connected to everything both here on Earth and across the stars and the universes. Loneliness disappears, becomes a non sequitur because we now know that we're always connected to everything in background mode, and now we're conscious of it. We can touch in there, feel the connections any time we want, without them intruding on what we're focusing on at any one time. 6-people are often closer to this realisation than others might be and become beacons of this knowing-consciousness for the rest of us to take light from.

6-people are about knowing, appropriate action, structuring ideas and visions, evoking knowing in others, and giving voice to intuition. Wise owls *know* this.

3-ness: Thinking/Reason

3 is the partner of 6. Draw the figure 3, quite snaky, isn't it? The pen moves in a half-moon curve clockwise, and then does it again. It's got a sort of Vroom! Vroom! rhythm. Draw it lots of times and get the feel into your body.

3-people are about thinking, intellect, reason, following patterns and maps, working things out, finding ways and paths, and very necessary qualities those are too. Without the thinking-function we wouldn't be able to get up on time, do arithmetic or maths, add up our bank accounts, drive the car, catch a train, do a shopping list, put our clothes on right, all that stuff. And we wouldn't be able to see a good argument from a bad one, reason a case, see flaws and falsehoods. It is our thinking, and our memory, which enable this, it's a very different thing from the *knowing* of 6-ness.

One of the things thinking is about is proof. Thinking has become very much the "god of our time". Schools and universities encourage those to whom thinking and reasoning come easy, those who pass exams, get degrees. Those sorts of folk also tend to function quite well within the rules of whatever society they live in, whereas people on the kenning, knowing, line can be very disruptive to normalcy. Instincts and knowing are not conducive to maintaining the status quo, 3-ness can be much easier to control.

We need reason, and we certainly shouldn't try to get rid of it, but we mustn't make it a god. Reason makes it possible to put ideas into words. The wise owl may be able to hoot but she needs a wider vocabulary than *Whoo! Whoo!* if non-owls are to understand her. Without the vocabulary, the owl is likely to be mobbed ... as is the owl in the everyday world when she comes out of her hole in the daytime. With reasoning-power, the owl is able to answer the questions which come from those to whom her ideas and philosophies are new.

Being a 3-person

3-people can easily get into the rut of over-thinking everything, of relying on thinking so much that the rest of their abilities, like empathy, knowing, feeling connected and grounded, love and emotions, the body and its senses, never get a look-in. Everything about them becomes *heady*, they refuse to do anything less it's somehow proven to them. This "proof" may often be simply to see the thing in print or on TV, or said by someone with alphabet soup after their name; they need "outside authority" to be able to accept something. The task for 3-people is to learn their own inner authority by getting in touch with their 6-ness side and the other numbers in their birth and name array. This will bring them out of their heads and into their whole selves. It can be a hard job because society so heavily encourages thinking as the be-all and end-all of everything, but they can do it once they put their minds to it and allow the rest of reality in.

The 3-person can also lose all ability to reason. They completely forget all the things they know about seeing falsity and inconsistency and go haring off after the "fact" without "rhyme or reason". This can make them very irritating to those around them and it can also be dangerous for both them and their companions. They will "follow the instructions" sometimes without taking the actual circumstances into account, so they lose touch with reality. For instance, if they are in a life-saving situation, they might as easily kill as cure if they act only on knowledge instead of the reality in front of them.

Risks can be another difficulty for 3-people. They may be very unwilling to take risks, to go beyond the known and to climb out of their box, so they don't allow themselves the opportunity to grow beyond what they already know. Risk enables us to show ourselves that we are very capable in situations we've not experienced before, that we can think on our feet, act both instinctively and intuitively, and so succeed where before we had feared to fail.

Descartes is quoted as saying, "I think, therefore I am". This has good and bad points. The power of the brain, of the electrical energy of the synapses, is a vital part of being but it is most certainly not its be-all. As so often in both life and magical work, it isn't possible to answer everything from within only one discipline, this is well shown in the mathematics of Kurt Gödel and his Theorems of Incompleteness, which shows that we need more than one branch of maths to come to full conclusions. Life and maths are inclusive not exclusive, and this is true of numerology as well. We cannot work ourselves fully and wholly within only one number, but 3-people may try to do this, to reduce their lives to just thinking. They may do this because it's less scary and more comfortable, makes life easier because everything can all be fitted into a normal-box. Doing this severely restricts them as they supress the other parts of themselves and, like with the other numbers, this suppression can cause physical and emotional illnesses.

On the other hand, when 3-people are balanced and inclusive, using all their numbers, they can provide the engine which will enable the knowing-bus to go.

3-ness is about giving ideas form and shape and colour ... see the torch exercise at the end of this book; it's about splitting light, and about how light is made up of the three primary colours, Newton's prism work. It shows you how when you put your hand between the light source and the wall, interrupting the flow of light and making shadows, you can then see the colours of the light, and its patterns. 3-ness is about all this, about interrupting the flow and creating the shadows which define things. The problem comes when the 3-person begins to think the shadow is the reality rather than just the form it has taken in order to be known.

Einstein told us that matter is highly compressed energy; this is a spiritual concept as well as one of physics. You might say matter is energy squeezed into form. The interruption of the light which creates colour and shadow is like this, it makes a form and shape for the light so that its various qualities can be seen. 3-ness is a way to do this. Reason is a means for clothing ideas in form so that they can be transmitted to others who haven't yet seen them or, at least, seen them in this particular way.

Being a head-set is another downside of 3-ness which you'll probably have already realised. Like 6-people, they can probably explain away anything, and talk the hind legs off a whole beachful of donkeys; 6-people and 3-people are alike in this but in a different way, this is part of the 3-6 partnership. 3-people usually sound very reasonable too so, if you're not good at this noticing this sort of thinking, they can easily side-track you off what you know into believing you've got the whole thing round the back of your neck. You'll likely end up agreeing with them, thanking them, perhaps even being in awe of them ... then you'll get home and feel seriously confused because your inner-knowing will be telling you everything your head has just got from this person is most definitely *not* how it is at all. And they do this to themselves as well. It's a form of painting yourself into a corner; you get so hedged about with reasons and rules and conventions and regulations that you can't see straight and haven't a clue how to get out of the mess. When it gets this bad the only way out is to cut the knot, crash the whole thing like the Tower in the Tarot, knock down the edifice of thinking and start again. Many politicians and spin-doctors are head-sets and desperately need to do this, and so do the rest of us voters as we may well have been completely befogged by their "science".

Being balanced in 3-ness is another very *and/and* place. You have the intellect to know the whys and wherefores of things, how they work and how to mend them, where they are, what they do, when they are, who they are and why they are ... the basic questions of How, Where, What, When, Who and Why. Admittedly, the why-question is often very difficult and the best way to come at its answer is through the other five, but this too is something the balanced 3-person realises. I said *realises*, meaning to make real, for themselves and others. This is a major 3-function, to make things real so that they can be seen and known by everyone. The wise owl 6-person may know a lot but not be able to put it over. The 3-person may be able to put anything over, sell coal to Newcastle as the old adage went, but not truly *know* a thing, only have the intellectual knowledge about it, book-learning not body-knowing. The balanced 3-person is able to know what they don't know, know where to find someone who does know it, and see how to put that knowing together in a way which can be seen.

3-people are also good at reason. They can see inconsistences, holes in theories, where someone hasn't been rigorous enough in their thinking. They may tend to say so-and-so has jumped to a conclusion in a derogatory way, perhaps because they don't yet have sufficient grasp of the knowing-principle of their intuition, but they can move past this. 3-ness isn't about intuition or direct knowing, gnosis, it's about giving this sometimes-formless stuff a form. 3-people can in-form. They put a form on an idea and so it informs people. They give structure.

So 3-people are an essential part of the mix, as are all the numbers, and without them the world doesn't work properly.

5 & 4 –Intuition and Instinct

5-times table			4-times table			
1x5=5		5	1x4=4			4
2x5=10	1+0=1	1	2x4=8			8
3x5=15	1+5=6	6	3x4=12	1+2=3		3
4x5=20	2+0=2	2	4x4=16	1+6=7		7
5x5=25	2+5=7	7	5x4=20	2+0=2		2
6x5=30	3+0=3	3	6x4=24	2+4=6		6
7x5=35	3+5=8	8	7x4=28	2+8=10	1+0=1	1
8x5=40	4+0=4	4	8x4=32	3+2=5		5
9x5=45	4+5=9	9	9x4=36	3+6=9		9

Figure 27: 5&4 tables

5	4
Star	Star
Crown	Base
Union	Connection
Spirit-Purpose	Intuition

Intuition and instinct are again two sides of one coin, and they connect the crown and the base chakras. They are like at each end of the vertical axis, apparent dichotomies but *not*, they're like the lady and lord again, the one is the other, but the other way up …

Figure 28: Lady & Lord

The same … but different. And each needs the other.

5-ness: Intuition

We'll begin, as usual, by drawing the figure 5. Draw it like this – begin with the down stroke, then form the moon-curve, and then take the pen off to put it back at the top and make the cross stroke. Do this several times ... da dee daaa, da dee daaa.

Feel into that rhythm, feel the straightness of the line, then the curve, then the lift-off in order to make a straight line in the opposite direction. Just let the doing of it float ideas and pictures into your mind.

What is Intuition?

Intuition is about having a hunch, an inkling, a sense or presentiment, the flash of an idea; it's also about your awareness and sensitivity, your ability to perceive a situation or how someone is feeling

It's often associated with *clairvoyance*, that word comes from the French and means to see clearly – think about that. Seeing clearly is about not having preconceptions, going into everything full of expectancy but without expectations, and seeing people and situations that way too. It's really hard to do because we're all brought up to think in the ways of our parents, family, school, friends, workplace, nation, politics, etc. Getting properly in touch with your intuition means you have to lose all those old habits and clean your slate. It's about WYSIWYG – What You See Is What You Get – and about that excellent catch-phrase, *doing what it says on the tin*.

So being clairvoyant means a lot more than looking into a dark mirror or crystal and seeing the future, or past, or a lover, or another place. It involves seeing clearly what is there, in front of you as well as what's in the mirror, and not translating it into what you would like it to be, or what fits with all your preconceptions.

Job & Spirit-Purpose

Intuition helps you to know, remember, your Spirit-Purpose, the job your spirit chose to do in this lifetime., the reason why your spirit chose to incarnate this time around.

There are no conscripts to life, only volunteers. We choose to incarnate each lifetime, nobody forces us to, it's something our spirit wishes to do. Incarnation has two main functions – the growth of our spirit, and to help the Earth and the universe in their overall plan. Each time we choose to incarnate, and well before we actually get born, we discuss what sort of job would be useful to the Earth, and our own growth, with the other members of our spirit family, what we call the *tylwyth* in the old British tongue.

Often, when we first arrive in incarnation (i.e. get born) we haven't a clue what our job is, not at first. This not-knowing can last for quite a long time; indeed some people never get a full handle on why they incarnated this time around. Sometimes, though, people do remember why they're here. Of famous people, the Dali Lama is one who comes into incarnation each time with full memory of previous lives as well as full knowing of what he's here to do this time around. Like I said, that can be very difficult ... even for him.

Most of us get a bad case of spiritual amnesia at birth, and for good reasons. It's not because we're unworthy, stupid, bad, or somehow "less", but because if we had retained the memory it would influence the choices we make, and so spoil the experiences our spirit knows it needs to have.

To remember why you incarnated can be equally difficult as not to remember. The human personality – the part that knows themselves only as Fred Blogs or Jane Doe – can be very strong in resisting the urges their spirit-selves to climb out of the comfortable box of not-knowing. When your spirit knows what you should be doing but your personality doesn't want to do it you can end up in quite a conflict.

Your spirit-self decides, before conception even, whether

this lifetime will begin with amnesia, partial remembering, or total recall. That might sound autocratic and overly parental but, remember, the spirit has a much wider, broader and deeper perspective of life, the universe and everything than our little personal-self will have. Indeed, it's the spirit-self that builds our body *and* our personality (our personal-self) for the purposes of the spirit-job it has chosen for that particular incarnation. We don't carry our personalities over across incarnations, they end along with our body's end at death, this is part of the reason many people fear death so much, because they only know it from the personality's perspective.

The personal-self, which while we're still unaware of our spirit seems to be the real and true "us", is only a tiny part of the story and is certainly not the driver of our bus. It doesn't know much about anything really until it begins to be aware of the spirit worlds. Sometimes, this is what the spirit needs. If the personal-self knows too much to begin with then it won't make the mistakes and choices that will enable us to grow.

The Arnold Schwarzenegger film "Total Recall" gives an idea of this, in fun and fantasy. The hero gets dreams and flashbacks of being another person. He gradually remembers more and more of "himself", then he sees an old film of himself talking to this person he is now, telling him that he is a *created personal-self*, made for a particular purpose. In the film the purpose is, of course, evil in order to make an exciting film, and so is the mastermind who helped created the self he now is. Arnie struggles against this and, of course, wins. He gains total recall of his true self, all the experiences which have made him who he is and, in consequence, saves the planet in true Schwarzenegger swashbuckling style.

This film is quite a good example of how it is for most of us although, hopefully, we don't all have quite such a trying and scary time as does Arnie in the film. But some of our wakeup-calls can be quite difficult and require us to grow and stretch a lot in order to handle them.

Your spirit is quite definitely *not* evil, but the personal-self's process of awakening to the spirit purpose is often similar to that of the hero in the film. It may well begin with dreams, flashbacks, knowing a place you've never been to before, and such like. If you follow up on those leads you uncover more and more of yourself. Some people resist, don't look, don't follow up and there's no compulsion from the spirit to do so. If you do go for it though then life really does open up enormously and become much more fun. People who know their spirit-purpose, at least to some extent, are never bored.

Ursula le Guin in LEFT HAND OF DARKNESS says ... *It's good to have an end to journey to but it's the journey that matters in the end.* This is such a true saying, and one we would all do well to put on post-it notes all round the house, and the office too. Life is a journey; the travels, adventures, difficulties, sorrows and joys are the meat of the journey. But it's good to have a destination to walk towards while taking one's time on the walk, and observing every twist and turn of the way. In Britain, one of the things we call our path is the twisted way; and this book is about your spiral dance with time ... another form of the twisting way. We journey along the paths of the City of Turns, the Caer y Troiau, so we come again to the city of windings or turnings, the Troytown.

Figure 29: Troytown

Your spirit-purpose is both that destination *and* the journey itself. You cannot do a "beam me up, Scottie" as they say in the

Star Trek films. You have to make your own way, noticing every footstep, every bump and lump in the path, all the beauty and all the ugliness of your journey too. Your spirit self needs you to know both; we're back to the two sides of one coin, the reality of duality yet again.

Being a 5-person

5-people are about living life to the full, and living out their life-purpose for each incarnation. To do this, they need to know that purpose as well as they possibly can, and also know that the journey to knowing their purpose will never end, not while they're still alive. They also know they will be learning and discovering all the way along that path, right up to the instant when they step back across the threshold out of incarnation and back into otherworld. That's quite a load to be aware of through your life.

Like many people, they will likely begin their life with the usual dose of spiritual amnesia, but they will also have a very strong pull, a persuasive and compelling itch, that will drive them towards finding their path. It's a sort of knowing that the everyday life they lead is quite definitely not all there is, and this itch, this knowing, will push them to discover and learn what their path is.

They're helped by the fact that they will naturally be an intuitive person, but their background, how they grew up, parents, school, and their current place in life, job and family, may inhibit them from realising this properly. Being intuitive often doesn't go down well in the everyday world, many people laugh at intuition, so intuitive folk may well be ridiculed within, and/or ostracised from, their peer group. That sort of treatment makes it very hard to live happily and contentedly in the everyday world, so the intuitive person may well hide within their cloak-of-pretending to be like everyone else. When this happens, the 5-person becomes inwardly conflicted, which doesn't bode well for them being able to realise themselves fully. They'll need help to find their way out of the conflict and into a place where they can be confident in being themselves. Not everyone finds the help they need.

But the itch will drive them. If they don't find outside help then the itch may well make them contact otherworld of themselves and ask spirit to help them. A strong 5-person will do this, even be demanding of spirit. To work directly with spirit is very strong and the results can be very quick. It may mean the person completely changes their whole life, jobs, home and maybe even relationships as well, seemingly almost overnight. Those around them may find this disruptive but that's no reason they should try to stop the person, however they feel about it. The 5-person needs to go on with their hunt for their path; if they don't they will give themselves all sorts of emotional and maybe mental difficulties. Their connection to spirit needs to be fulfilled in their everyday life.

Seeking out one's spirit-purpose is not a selfish pursuit although those around you may perceive it as such because you may not take as much notice of them as they would like. Sometimes, when you begin on this path, you do become obsessed as I said before, and so may behave like a child who hasn't yet grasped that they are not the centre of the universe. 5-people need to learn to look at themselves and see themselves clearly; remember this is what *clairvoyance* means in French. They may think they have it, because it looks good and fits the current thinking-box, so they gallop at it at full tilt; objectivity goes right out the window. They need to learn to sit on their hands, stop, stand back, ponder, sit-with, wait – and waiting is sometimes the hardest thing in the world to do. They need to take notice of everything on the path, not just humans but all the rest of life too – this will give them a wider and deeper view of their place in the total scheme of things.

Because they understand about the itch, the dream, the search for meaning, 5-people can help others in the same boat. Their ability to speak out of themselves rather than out of a book gives them authenticity; it's much easier to hear and understand people who are authentic. Authenticity is good for everyone, not just 5-people; they can help others to find their own knowing (kenning).

4-ness: Instinct

We'll begin, as usual, by drawing the figure 4. People usually begin by drawing the moon-shaped down stroke; it's the same sort of shape as the waxing crescent of the moon …

Figure 30: waxing crescent moon

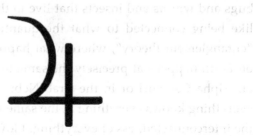

Figure 31: number 4

After the curve of the moon, head off horizontally to the right, to draw the horizontal stroke, then the pen comes off and makes the vertical down-stroke to cross the horizontal. So the figure 4 contains the waxing crescent moon, the vertical axis and the horizontal axis … like the figure 5 but drawn differently and producing a different shape.

The 4 begins with the moon-shape, then the horizontal, and finally the vertical down-stroke. The 5 begins with the vertical down-stroke, then the moon-shape, and finally the horizontal.

Do the figure 4 several times ... daaa dee, daaa dee dee. Feel into that rhythm, feel the curve, then the straightness of the horizontal line, then the lift-off in order to make the vertical down-stroke. Just let the doing of it float ideas and pictures into your mind.

So what is instinct?

Instinct is what comes naturally, what's in your makeup, your predisposition and what drives you. It's about your natural talents and gifts, aptitudes, having a knack and a flare for something. It's also the wordless "gut feeling" when we know something and, however sophisticated we may feel ourselves to be, we often find that our gut was right.

It's like having a connection to the threads of the universe, of this Earth – what the scientists call mycorrhiza, the mycelia that connect plants, and soil, and water, and carbon, and all the bugs and worms and insects that live in the soil. In physics, it's like being connected to what the quantum particle guys call "entanglement theory", where what happens to a particle here on Earth happens at precisely the same instant to its co-particle on Alpha Centauri or in the Crab Nebula. Distance no object, everything knows everything at the same instant, an example of the interconnectedness of everything. I love the way at-the-edge physics so often says what we say in the way of the shaman.

The mycorrhiza help us relate to intuition and instinct very well as the mycelia are physical things that we can actually look at, whereas energy connections, the energy threads, may seem very out of this world.

Both 4 and the 5 people have these connections closer to their fingertips than others may do; this can be both a blessing and a curse.

Being a 4-person

The 4-person has a very strong connection with the Earth. Like the mycorrhiza who connect the plants through the soil, the skin, of the Earth, the 4-person is able to feel the threads that connect them to all the rest of life on the Planet.

This knowing through the threads of the Earth can be difficult for 4-people as not too many other folk have this ability, so they, like 5-people, may suppress the knowing. 4-people are pulled two ways, into being who they truly are and at the same time towards conforming with the rest of society; this latter, for them, is living a lie. Like 5-people they have to find their own way into "being real" but, while the 5-person has the intolerable itch to discover their path the 4-person may have the reverse, an incredible urge to hide, stay underground and not come out. It's certainly possible to live like this and many do, but it's not possible to fulfil your path this way, and it leads to physical and emotional stress which can cause illness.

In the 21st century we're not encouraged to use our instincts or develop our intuitive powers. Westernised society prefers folk live in a world where things are proven through the intellect; this naturally limits what it's possible for us to know unless it already fits inside the intellect-box. Using instincts and intuition isn't considered good practice, and is often thought to be old-fashioned and superstitious. Statistics rarely work with instincts or intuition and modern western civilisation is largely ruled by statistics. Life can be hard for 4 and 5 people. Knowing-in-your-bones and hunches are not normal, and anyway they're just "coincidences".

Let's look at the word coincidence … it comes from the verb "to coincide" which means to match, correspond, and is about things that happen together. It's similar to synchronicity and synchronous, things happening, existing or arising at the same time. Modern everyday thinking has come to translate all this as *accident*, assuming there's no logical thinking behind it. People find it disturbing to think that things can happen at the same time without them knowing why – like the particles in entanglement theory – and so choose to believe that such things do not and cannot happen.

4-people are in touch with their instincts and unlikely to be scared by that, but they may be scared by other people's reaction to them. Indeed, 4-people themselves may appear scary to those who don't know or use their instincts, particularly when 4-people see things very quickly and as a whole, without having to make the (to them) wearisome journey from a-b-c-d-etc. as the intellectual linear thinker does.

Geniuses have a strong instincts and intuition and may have 4 very strongly in their numbers. Albert Einstein did, the numbers for each of his names add to 4, Albert being 22 and Einstein being 40. His genius-quality was in being able to make connections, see threads, so he drew things together into his general and special theories of relativity which have transformed how we know our world, the universe and everything.

Using instinct and intuition enables you to see the threads, both the physical threads like the mycorrhiza, and the energy threads. You tend to see things whole, all of a piece and all to once. Using the intellect to see the interconnectedness of things is very hard work. Things just don't connect in long linear two-dimensional chains, they connect in three-dimensional webs. Computers are intellectual things that "think" in a linear fashion, although software engineers are now attempting to stretch this further into webs, but the strict linearity is how computers can get apparently obvious (to us) things wrong. School, and sometimes university, thinking can encourage the easily-provable linear mode (complete with footnotes), this is very hard work for those who work instinctively and intuitively to either do or understand. Inappropriate use of and emphasis on computers can encourage people to try to think like them, with disastrous results. Minds do not function like computers.

4-people see things first without having to reason out how to do it, they go backwards later to find ways to show other people what they discover. They're walkers between worlds, knowing thisworld and otherworld and being able to cross between them.

These qualities need training and understanding. If you're a 4-person and feel the urge to walk between worlds, find yourself a good, experienced teacher to travel and journey with. Such a person won't be one who quotes rules but one who encourages you to discover your own inner knowing and to work with it. Unfortunately, such teachers do not grow on every bush, nor are there many of them to the pound. Beware of teachers who encourage you to work with them! The best teachers will probably do their best to talk you out of it, be busy all the time, tell you how bad it will be, suggest you don't bother and possibly even be quite rude. When you find one of these, stick like glue as you'll have struck gold. These sorts of folk really do know the way, they really can go out and come home again, bringing the goodies with them unchanged, and they really can rescue you if (when) you get into trouble as you assuredly will. They will likely lead you up and down the garden path too, for good walkers between worlds are also rocket-science tricksters, it goes with the territory. They are also extremely good fun to be with, very compassionate, caring, honest and truthful.

Because 4-people can see the interconnectedness of everything at first hand they will have equal compassion for a cat, computer or child, their car, a carrot, and everything from the tiniest particle, atom and microbe to the hugest mountain and the Earth herself. They find it impossible to be "humans first", it's a non-sequitur for them, makes no sense. They see the life-energy in everything and how it's the same in everything, so how could life-energy in one particular form be superior to another? They know that the matter which makes up their own bodies is the same matter that makes up their car, or a star, so how can they care more for matter in one form than in another?

This can be a hard place to live in many societies. Most people care for humans first, before everything else, and feel themselves to be separate from other life-forms, and from the planet Earth herself, and from the stars. 4-people have to learn to live in this society which, if they come out with what they know, will think them stupid and crazy, and shun them. They may become very depressed if they have to endure this. It's hard to live a lie, to pretend you are something you're not, to hide, and to still have to listen to and live with what is to you, crazy talk.

Words that spring to mind for the balanced and integrated 4-person include laughter. They will have a wicked sense of humour combined with a very honest and genuine compassion. And they can "fly" with both feet still securely on the ground, which sounds like a paradox but think about it. The 4-person is wholly connected to the Earth and is also, at the same time, able to walk in otherworld. They're like a connector, a "bridge" between the two.

They may well choose work that connects them to the Earth, possibly something as mundane-seeming as gardening or maybe in more of an educative capacity, maybe even social work. They need to take care not to let themselves become a guru; this may be very difficult when they're good at their job. Followers are not really useful, but helping folk to open their eyes to their own reality is.

4-people are good at reality, real reality, it's the 4-square aspect of themselves, so when they're integrated and balanced they're also well grounded. They're unlikely to be worried when reality doesn't look how it says it should in the book, or when it appears frightening. They know that reality is the unknown, what's around the corner, the edge, and that it's their instinctual link, the touch of the threads, that gives them a bridge to it. They may seem unusual to others but there is a warmth about them which carries people over the gulf of dissimilar thinking.

9 & 0 – Infinitely Small & Infinitely Huge

Nine and zero are different to the other numbers ... there are 9-people but there cannot be any Zero people of course. Let's look at the 9 times table first to help understand this a bit further, we'll go on to look at the 0 times table after.

9-times table

1x9=9		9
2x9=18	1+8=9	9
3x9=27	2+7=9	9
4x9=36	3+6=9	9
5x9=45	4+5=9	9
6x9=54	5+4=9	9
7x9=63	6+3=9	9
8x9=72	7+2=9	9
9x9=81	8+1=9	9

Figure 32: 9 table

As you see, both numbers only ever reduce to themselves. This is a fundamental thing about them which is significant when you work with them. And both are important even though the idea of working with zero may, at first, seem very weird.

Do you see that each multiplication of 9 gives us one of the pairs of numbers?

1&8, 2&7, 3&6, 4&5 ... and then reversing the pairs 5&4, 6&3, 7&2, 8&1.

If you go down the left-hand numbers of the product (i.e. multiplication) of each multiplication you get 1,2,3,4,5,6,7,8; then if you go down the right-hand numbers of the product you get 8,7,6,5,4,3,2,1. Again each column reverses the other. Do this table for yourself now, doing it helps bring the knowing of it into your bones.

There seems to be quite a pattern here, doesn't there? And it's all about reversals, one going one way while its partner goes the other: one goes up the other goes down. We're back on that double spiral, deosil and widdershins, yet again. Duality rules OK, and 9 is particularly good at showing you this.

Zero times

Now let's play with zero.

10 times anything just adds a zero to the number, in maths this is called *going up an order of magnitude* ... 10x5=50 or 10x4=40. The number you were multiplying moves a pace to the left, very basically that's what *order of magnitude* is, and that is extremely important when you work with your numbers.

So 10 times anything when added down, reduced, reverts to the original number, e.g. 5+0=5 and 4+0=4, so it becomes 1 times whatever number, i.e. itself. The zero disappears and you are left with only the number you were first working with. This too is important when working with your numbers.

So ... *up* an order of magnitude means up a turn of the spiral, and *down* an order of magnitude means down a turn of the spiral; it's one of the keys to the evolutionary and inward properties of the numbers.

Although all this sounds rather heady and mind-boggling it really does all work out beautifully. Stay with me and hang in there ...

Patterns

Let's look at them further.

If you add any number to nine and then reduce it back down, you always get the number you first thought of ... the 9 disappears; it's as if the nine is *invisible*.

5+9 = 14 so 1+4 = 5

Try it for yourself, you'll find that whatever number you add to the 9, and however many 9s you put in, the 9 always disappears. It holds the invisible power.

Another nice trick of the 9-times table is how it creates the pairs of numbers and reverses them, so showing them to us as both the inward and outward spirals.

9 is a fundamental and invisible power behind the other numbers when it occurs in a chart. It holds all of them in their pairs, and so holds the pattern of duality.

9 requires to be broken down into the pairs in order to create a pattern. Of itself, 9 is the dot, it's that hydrogen atom that sparks off life by becoming helium in the sun; it gives power to all the numbers.

In order to move, to create the pattern of life, 9 *splits* into the other numbers, like white light splits in the rainbow colours and refracts through the prism. White light is both white *and* contains all the colours, and/and, it too contains that double spiral, that duality, that enables life.

Look at this table. The left-hand column is the *mirror* image of the right-hand one. Mirror is another important concept when you work with your numbers. It's a large part of the function zero but it occurs in a hidden way for 9 too.

09	90
18	81
27	72
36	63
45	54

Figure 33: 9 mirror table

Now, look at these two columns of numbers – the numbers from zero to nine and nine to zero written out in two columns. What have you got? The result, the product, of the 9-times table.

0	9
1	8
2	7
3	6
4	5
5	4
6	3
7	2
8	1

Figure 34: 9 result table

I'm labouring this quite heavily here because by actually doing and looking at it in this way all these concepts become real to you, you begin to get them into your bones. This way you come to know of yourself, by doing, that 9 *holds* the powers of the double spiral of inward and outward movement. It is *the hidden power* of the labyrinth.

Hmm! 9 is a pretty subtle number and so too is Zero. It too is somewhat invisible, not in the same ways as 9. Whatever you add, subtract, multiply or divide it with or to you still end up with zero, nothing, no-thing; so zero is very much about no-thing-ness. In containing no particular thing, *it contains the potential for all things.*

Dots & Circles

Let's play with dots and circles, and putting them together to help us understand 9 and zero further.

We'll use the numbers circle again for the 9-times table.

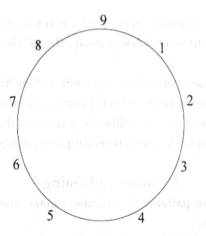

Figure 35: n umbers circle

So let's do it, put your pen on the 9 and keep doing it for each line of the table as you did for the others. It just keeps on dotting on the figure nine, it doesn't make the usual inward and evolutionary circles. And the zero doesn't even appear on the numbers circle at all so it shows you by its non-existence that it's about *no-thing* and express that as a circle.

If you then put the symbols for 9 and 0 together, as a picture, you get the glyph for the sun. This is what the 9 and the 0 are about, the power of the sun which enables Life.

Figure 36: sun glyph

Nine is the power that *enables* the sun. It's symbolised by the dot at the centre which is the glyph for our sun. our sun is a *continuous* nuclear fusion reaction that gives us our energy, our light and heat, and so enables photosynthesis which is the basis for all life.

Zero holds and transmits that power, rather like the gravity and electromagnetic fields which hold and enable the nuclear fusion in the sun. Gravity holds the Earth in orbit around our life-giving star so we keep on receiving that energy.

Drawing and Doing

You've drawn the patterns the numbers make, the inwards and outwards spirals.

Drawing the patterns, and physically doing the times-tables, puts the sensation of them *into your body*, begins your body-knowing of the numbers which is very important. It's important to understand numerology intellectually but you will never *know* it until you also acquire the body-knowing, know it in your bones.

Body-knowing, knowing something in your bones is an instinctual process. As you become physically accustomed to working with your instinct, through body-knowing enabled by drawing, this ability enables your intuition to function (remember about the 5/4 pair). It also helps you to be aware of both your instinct and your intuition and to tell them apart; this is important because they often get confused with wishful thinking and neither instinct nor intuition are that. This is where body-knowing helps you. Your body doesn't work with the intellectual intricacies that your brain does. It knows when it's wet, hot, thirsty, hungry, sexy, tired, excited, it doesn't need to intellectualise about these things, it just *knows* them. Through sensations, it can show you when you are working authentically, using your instinct and intuition, and when you're kidding yourself, but you need to learn its language to do this.

The purpose of getting in touch with your numbers, and learning to work with them, is to become a complete and spirit-conscious person. To do this we need both our birth and our name numbers. Our numbers show us who we are, what we want to do to help the earth, how to become part of the team, how to make ourselves the best spirit-conscious person we can manage. We become artists of the Self and the self.

9 & 0 – the Void and the Sun

Now you have the basic concepts of the 9 and zero we'll go on to talk about them and how they dance together.

9	0
Star	Star
Void	Sun
Will	Mirror
Act of Completion	Completeness
Invisible force	Container of force – Cauldron
Sperm	Egg

9-ness: The Void

A major attribute of 9 is that once you've reached it you go up an order of magnitude, go onto another turn of the spiral, get larger by more than the sum of your parts; 9 is the stepping stone to another level. It also means that having achieved the top of one ladder you go find yourself at the bottom of the next one.

The number 9 is related to the king of the Underworld who, in many traditions, has a *cap of darkness* and a *cauldron* amongst his treasures. The cap of darkness is the cap of invisibility, one of nine's major attributes. Another wearer of this cap is Hermes, Mercury, the messenger and Trickster god of communication who also symbolises the interconnectedness of all life threads. He works through the flowing, liquid metal of quicksilver. Hermes is also perhaps much earlier a god of northern Europe associated with Gaul from the Roman writings; he is similar to Llew from the Brythonic tradition and Lugh from Irish myth, a sun, storm and sky god.

This tells us something about the wearer of the cap of darkness, and about how we may use the ideas he shows us in working with our numbers. The underworld is the place of the ancestors for most shamanic traditions, the place of stored experience and the wisdom that can be drawn from there. The number 9 also has the power-qualities of a black hole in that no light can escape from a black hole because of its immense gravitational field – another way of being invisible. It also has worm-hole qualities of communication across otherwise impossible boundaries, a dimension-changing ability. 9 enables communication across the worlds, across space-time, across the realms and kingdoms of nature, including stars and universes as well as spiritual kingdoms.

9 makes change happen. It's the will and the power, but not power over. This is enabling power, the *power to enable* ... power to love, power to help, power to care, and the will to good. Some people call this the "will to *do* good" but that's not right, the "will to *do* good" can land you in all sorts of trouble as it lets in your brain which gets on the job of telling you just what doing good is! The will to do good often means doing what you *think* is best and, usually, without asking the recipient if what you're going to do is of the least use to them at all, or will actually make things worse!

On the other hand, the *will to good* is about asking otherworld to help you do the *appropriate* thing, in the appropriate place at the appropriate time. Appropriate is the way to get things right. The will to good never knows best, and is open to outcomes it had never dreamed of ... a very different thing.

Drawing the number 9

Now, practical stuff. Draw a simple 9 like in the picture.

Figure 37: number 9

Your pen does two things, first it goes round in a widdershins circle, then it goes downwards in a straight line. So 9 is made of a circle and a line, it holds two ideas, both of which are never ending in their own ways.

When you draw it, you arbitrarily decide to begin and finish drawing a circle at a particular point. Similarly, you decide to begin and end the straight line. The line could go on forever in both directions but it doesn't, it finishes, becomes complete, as does the circle. So in drawing 9, you are drawing two versions of eternity, the circle and the line, and combining them together … another *and/and* concept. That says a lot about the qualities of 9. Enabling power is inclusive, not separatist.

Spend some time drawing nines. Nine has a rhythm too, dee-da, dee-da, uneven, it has movement, as you stop you want to start again. We all write sloppily some of the time but there's something of an innate need to complete the figure nine which expresses 9-ness, it's a number of completion, the act of completion, and, at the same time, the will to begin again.

What are 9-people about?

9-people are instruments of change, transformation and sometimes transmutation as well, they make radical changes happen around them. They often appear magical and formidable and extraordinary. On the downside, this can be intimidating so 9-people need to learn to keep their cloak of invisibility around them so that others may be comfortable. They have the ability to find and achieve their path much more easily than most people, they may even have knowing of their birth and even their conception, they may also awake in the womb. This latter can be very disconcerting – imagine finding yourself confined in a dark lake with perhaps your most recent memory is of playing in otherworld. However, 9-people are often also gifted with the ability to reach across space-time to get help from otherworld to remain sane in this amazing situation. This shows the remarkableness of 9-people.

On the downside, they can slip into the place of "power over" with dreadful consequences. They are power-full. An interesting example of this downside is Hitler. We know him as Hitler rather than Adolf Hitler, if we add up this name we find Hitler adds to 9, and Hitler was indeed powerful. He was not about enabling power though, he used his power to manifest his exclusive and racist dreams and came far too close for comfort in succeeding.

I'm most certainly not suggesting all 9-people are like this, indeed most of them are not at all and are far more in tune with enabling others, but I am saying that the power of 9 is strong enough to produce this. 9-people need to become very self-aware and self-actualised so they know what they're doing.

Zero-ness: The Sun

This number is a whole other ballgame to any of the others. As we've seen, there can be any zero-people, but zero is extremely powerful wherever it appears in your numbers.

Zero is about the inexpressible, about eternity and continuity. We, our spirit-selves, don't end when our current body dies. If you consider it biologically every cell in your body has died and been replaced many times by the time you are just seven years old, so by the time you're three-score-years-and-ten all the cells in your body have been replaced many times over. But all this time you remain. You, your spirit-self, are not the cells of your body, you are the spirit which *inhabits* that body. The process of cells dying and replacing themselves continues all your life; when you vacuum up the dust as you clean house much of that dust is your own dead body-cells. But *you* still remain. The cells of your body are *not* the essential you.

The real you, the spirit-you, is part of what the Zero is about, that continuity.

Now ... don't go panicking that you have no continuity if you have no zeros in your birth or name numbers. It doesn't work like that. Stay with me and keep on reading.

The zero holds the energies of the sun, our personal star here on Planet Earth. The sun is the light-bringer, energy and life giver. Without the sun we wouldn't exist.

The sun is also a wonderful maelstrom of enormous energies. It's a nuclear fusion bomb continually going off – NOTE, *fusion* not fission! Fusion is the bringing together of things, fission is blowing them apart. This is very significant. The sun is about bringing together, one of the functions of love. It is through this function that it enables life to *be*.

The sun gives light, which enables us to see, both physically and etherically, so we can see the visible wart on our friend's nose *and* the etheric wart on their personal-self. This can be uncomfortable for all parties and is a trait to be used with great compassion so don't shoot your mouth off just because you can see a hole in someone's shoe, or in their personal-self.

People with zeros are mirrors. They reflect back what they see, another uncomfortable trait. Sometimes their mirror is too bright, too clear, and so blinds the person it is reflecting, which is disabling, one of the down-sides of the zero.

Draw a zero. Draw lots of zeros. Get the feel of zero into your body. Now, what happens to your *feelings* as you draw this figure?

The circular path is one which human beings naturally wish

to follow. There is a strong "there and back again" feel to the zero, like Bilbo's journey in THE HOBBIT, and Bilbo is very happy to return, to come home. He is less happy that home isn't quite the same as it was before he went, but that is how it always is. There are lots of adages from around the world which express this such as *"You can't step into the same river twice"* but I like the Ursula Le Guin quote from THE DISPOSSESSED very much ...

You can go home again, the General Temporal Theory asserts, so long as you understand that home is a place you have never yet been.

Even on the circular path, home is not the same as it was when you left. On the spiral path, the way of the universe, it is different again ... and yet more the same. You land 'above' where home was on your original circle, so you now have a different perspective on it, one of distance and time, what science calls space-time, than you did when you were last at this place. You now have more past, your universe has got larger. You don't have to try to go back to being the person you were when you left home, which is impossible anyway; you can now be the enlarged person your life-journey has helped you become. So home is the same *and* different, but is not a place you have ever been before.

The zero becomes a spiral. Try drawing the zero becoming spiral in the air now, not on paper, allowing your hand to rise with each turn. How does this feel?

The Spiral Dance

Figure 38: double spiral

The pairs of numbers dance upwards and downwards, inwards and outwards, making the double-spiral of life and, in doing so, they can help you learn more about yourself and why you're here in incarnation on the Earth right now. The different, opposite, directions of the numbers, tell you about your spirit-self and your personal-self. They help you learn how to weave these two selves together, so becoming a whole person.

The numbers and qualities of each self are ...

Spirit Self	Personal Self
8 = ancestors	1 = Sensory body
7 = Love-Wisdom	2 = Feelings
6 = Knowing	3 = Thinking
5 = Intuition	4 = Instinct

As you've already seen, each of these pairs of numbers adds to 9, and 9 is the deep root number which pairs with the zero, the invisible power within all the pairs of numbers.

The numbers, because they work in pairs like this, each hold half of the whole, like two sides of one coin. They're not *either/or*, they're not about *either* the spirit *or* the personal-self, they're about *both* working together. Both are necessary. Spirit, on its own, cannot work with matter, it cannot function on its own in our everyday world but needs the personal-self to help it do that. You really do need your personal-self, it's not something nasty to be got rid of; the numbers help you learn this, and to understand the traits, strengths and weaknesses you designed into yourself for this current incarnation. Knowing this, you can do, and enjoy, the job you promised otherworld you'd do in this current incarnation.

Spiral Path

Numerology doesn't end when you're born, it's happening all the time. The nine-year cycles are part of the spiral of life which affects us and from which we can learn much.

Decades – 2000-2009 is an overall decade of the zero; 2010-2019 is a decade of 1-ness; 2020-2029 is a decade of 2-ness; and so it goes on as each decade changes in each century.

Anyone older than nine years will have done decade-cycles before, but it usually takes more life-experience to come to notice, and maybe later in life, to understand them.

In the past people will have done a zero-decade before – 1900-1909 – but that's not like 2000-2009 because there hasn't been a year 2009 in anyone's life. Or our recorded history, which is worth thinking about. Are you getting the hang of how everything changes, becomes new, while at the same time retaining some recognisable landmarks?

Of course, the Earth is very much older than two thousand years, but the particular cycle we are living in at the moment was conditioned and numbered by the emergence of Christianity, and the calendars we use nowadays are built on this. Although other traditions number things differently, according to their own histories, as a whole world we are living within the Christian-calendar tradition. Think about it, if you catch a plane from London to Hong Kong you don't suddenly find yourself in a different year when you land. The Hong Kong newspapers will still have the same date on them that the London ones do ... the

Hong Kong stock market wouldn't do business else. So like it or not, we are living in the Christian-calendar era.

This moving up of the numbers each decade, moves us up an order of magnitude, which is how the spiral works. If this feels difficult still, go back to making the circle-becoming-a-spiral with your hand in the air. Feel again how your hand moves; likely it moves both upwards and outwards, it includes more space, and more time, as you continue to do the movement. When you've done this for a little while, get a cup of tea and sit-with the feelings and sensations doing it gave you; ponder on it for a while, allow it to begin to show you what this spiral movement is about.

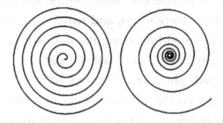

Figure 39: linear & exponential spirals

Now ponder on the idea of the linear spiral and the exponential spirals – do you see the difference between them? It's both a spatial and a linear difference. Try doing each of the spiral with your hand so you can *feel* the difference. Look at the two drawings, does one of them give you the feel of disappearing down a hole?

If life was like the linear spiral picture we wouldn't change, we'd stay the same. But it isn't, it's like the exponential spiral; each turn gets larger and more inclusive, and so we evolve. The Earth, the Solar System, the Milky Way galaxy and the Universe all evolve in that way too. All life follows the exponential spiral.

There are three conceptual paths human beings can follow ...

- the *straight* or linear path with past behind you, future in front of you

- the *circular* path where you tread around the route, returning to places, situations you've been to before
- the *spiral* where you return to places which are similar to those you've been before but the new place now includes all you've learned since the last time a situation like this turned up – so neither it nor you are the same as last time. This is the spiral path, it's never the same place or situation when you come to it again. You have grown, you are able to respond differently and, by doing so, you enable space-time to grow too.

The *linear* path keeps you very much in the space-time of your current incarnation; there's you, and where you have been, and where you will be, plodding along the path with only past and future for company ... neither of which exist.

The *circular* path gives you glimpses of new ways of doing things but basically you're still on the same old path, going round and round. You begin to see cycles as things to repeat but you don't yet grasp that they're also different. You get glimpses of an otherworld, of life beyond what you know from the everyday, but that too seems a stable place that goes round and round the same old cycles. You don't yet go forward into the truly new.

The *spiral* path is always both the same and different. As I said above, the Ursula Le Guin passage from her novel, The Dispossessed: *You can go home again ... so long as you understand that home is a place where you have never been* puts it very well. We are still travelling the spiral, as when I quoted Le Guin previously; home is a previous turn of the spiral. This is such a beautiful lesson and we all need to learn it. It's the way to grow and become more inclusive, and so more connected to all the other worlds.

People begin their evolution on the linear path. It's very personal, they believe they progress from a to b to c, like an orderly time-line. Later, they begin to feel the connectedness of everything, and also to sense the *homecoming* which is so reassuring at the end of our lives. We see our life as a circle, a bit like Bilbo with his there and back again. We go out on a journey and return home.

Later still, we begin to understand that we can only truly go home when we realise, as Le Guin says, that home is a place we have never yet been ... because the individual who returns home is *not* the same one who went out. The homecoming individual brings with them all they've gleaned from living, and maybe also what they remember from other incarnations too, to add to the store of knowing held by the home. So they come to know the spiral path, for the home they return to is not the one they left, nor are they the same being who returns to it.

This can be a difficult concept to accept because it shows, unutterably, the impermanence of things and people. It shows you can never go back. It makes us know that loss is real and always, always happens. The child or teenager or young adult can no longer play in the garden, in paradise. Now the garden has to include the whole world. Eventually it will include the whole of creation.

So the child-spirit walks the straight path. The young-adult-spirit walks the circular path. The mature spirit walks the spiral path.

Time Spirals

Numerology is a very powerful tool and numbers are one of our connections to the universe. Numerologists use numbers to discover how people work, what makes them tick, because numbers are a code for life. Scientists at SETI (Search for Extra-Terrestrial Intelligence) send out messages to the rest of the universe made out of numbers because they are a shorthand or code which seems likely to be understood throughout the universe. Scientists also use numbers, maths, to communicate ideas to each other; they've also found that the laws of physics make sense and are communicable through numbers.

Numbers and ratios describe relationships between things, and those relationships exist beyond human invention. For instance, the distance between the Earth and the Sun is so many miles, kilometres, light-years, whatever you like to name the scale of numbers. The name doesn't make the number; it merely describes it and gives it a form which we can use; the distance was there before there were any human beings to give names to things. That distance changes a little all the time too. The Earth is not the same distance from the Sun now as she was at the beginning of her life 4.5-odd billion years ago; according to current science it seems we're moving away from the sun at about 15cm/year – no big deal, you say! No, not in the tiny, short lifetime of a human, but try doing the sum 15cm x 5 billion; from the Earth's perspective, it's quite a bit, and she's not even half way through her lifetime, or so science thinks. Numbers tell us things about the world we live in, about the universe we live in.

Human beings have spent most of their collective lives, maybe three million Earth-years (that's just a mere 1/1500th of the Earth's lifetime), *working with* our home-planet, Mother Earth. Then, in the very recent past, just a mere 10 to 6 thousand years ago depending where you live, we changed and ceased to *work with* her but began to try to *control* her. We discovered/invented agriculture and brought enormous changes to the way we live, to our culture, to the concepts of our relationship with the Earth and all her creatures, and with each other, all of which have affected and still are affecting our Mother Earth disastrously. We need to turn our attitudes around and learn again how to *live with* the Earth rather than exploit her for our selfish wants.

Turning around doesn't mean going back – that's never possible – but it does mean we can change how we think, change our attitudes and how we live, so we can again put the needs of the Earth before our own personal wants. It's a difficult thing to do, especially nowadays when everything and everyone is telling you that you and your ego are the most important thing since sliced cat-food! That ego-idea also makes us fear that no one will look out for us, that we will suffer if push comes to shove, even from our nearest and dearest. Many people feel desperately alone – nobody really cares about me, when it comes down to it, there's only me; this only encourages them to further grasp onto everything they have, hang on tight, and grab anything else they see as well, even when it belongs to someone else – what's yours is mine, and what's mine is my own. People so easily become greedy and selfish.

Understanding what our numbers tell us about our lives, and the choices that are possible for us, can help us make this change. They show us a far bigger picture of life, the universe and everything, than the one most people usually have from ordinary, everyday living. Again, many people have come to feel pretty much powerless to do anything to make any changes, so they struggle on in the same old rut, unable to see a way out, a way to change. Numbers can help us discover ways to change and as we see ourselves change, through working with our numbers, so we come to know that we are able to make changes which go beyond ourselves to help the Earth as well.

As we come to learn, to know-in-our-bones, that we chose to be born for a real and useful purpose, we are able to let go of that helpless feeling. We understand what we're doing and are able to interact positively with life rather than lying down like a doormat and letting it all happen to us. We begin to see the wider purpose, the purpose that goes beyond our little personal self, and this in its turn this helps us know we're part of the whole ... and not just part of the human whole but part of *everything* on Earth, and the stars and the universe too.

Numbers empower us. They show us we're part of the wonderful dance of time. Once you begin to know for certain that this current life is not all there is, you feel less pressured to squeeze the most out of everything, right now, for yourself. You appreciate the joy of beginning things that will not come to fruition until long after the body you're currently wearing is dead and gone. You even realise that you may come back in a future incarnation and see it. Reincarnation becomes a fact of life.

This has wonderful repercussions. If you're going to reincarnate many times, then it's extremely likely you'll walk into the resultant mess that some of your previous behaviour has initiated. Eastern philosophies call this karma, but our own natural philosopher, alchemist and the grandfather of modern science, Sir Albert Newton, had a different and (to me) much more understandable way of putting it. He said, "*Every action has an equal and opposite reaction.*" Same thing.

Once you realise this you also realise it's an excellent reason for *not* behaving badly in the first place; many humans are coming to know this now and it's helping them understand there's much more life than they had thought. One of the extras that comes to most people once they start to live this way is that what they've cheerfully called inanimate objects might well not be so after all. As you get into a deeper relationship with the universe, by understanding your own space-time place in it better through your numbers, you start to see there's spirit, anima, in every form, molecule, atom and particle, whether it's in the shape of a bank manager, a fox, a fir tree, or a fridge. It's even there in a cabbage, and so becomes part of you after you've eaten it! The old song, *On Ilkley Moor Baht' At*, tells the sequence perfectly, and shows us the interconnectedness of all life.

Your numbers provide the clues to the pattern of the incarnation you're currently living. Knowing this pattern helps you to bring it to consciousness and so make it real, make it happen in your everyday life. Coming to this real consciousness can be difficult and painful but, until you do, you haven't a chance of becoming whole. We all need to become conscious.

Time

Time is different for all of us. This diagram gives the spirals of time as we know it.

Figure 40: time spirals

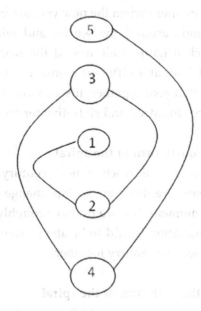

1 = Day: the inmost point of the spiral

Monday doesn't happen at the same time all around the Earth. When your Monday begins depends on the degree of longitude where you live, and maybe the moment the sun rises in your part of the world. Monday, for you in London, doesn't begin at the same time as it does for your friends in New York, Mexico City, Sydney or Cape Town ... or even for your friends in Paris. Our time, our days, are always wholly related to where we live.

2 = Month: the second turn of the spiral

June doesn't begin at the same time for you and all of your friends around the world either. However, it's a much longer period, thirty whole days-worth, so all around the world we get to experience most of June together, at roughly the same time, even if it's not precisely the same moment.

3 = Year: the third turn of the spiral

Every year we all have new year celebrations, new calendars. Again, the actual moment when the new year arrives is different for all those friends around the world, and with global TV we can now watch it happen all around the world and really experience that it *is* all at a different moment to us. And we all get to experience that year together, it's a communal experience for most of its three hundred and sixty-five (or six) days.

4 = Century: the fourth turn of the spiral

Every hundred years we reach a new century. Again, just like with new years, we don't all do this change of century at exactly the same moment. But we do have roughly four human generations (a generation is said to be about twenty-five years) in which to experience a century together.

5 = Millennium: the fifth turn of the spiral

At the beginning of the year 2000 we got to experience three things at once ... a new year, a new century and a new millennium. A millennium means one thousand years. Again, all the millennium parties began at their own individual moments when that part of the Earth literally moved into the new year, century and millennium. A thousand years is far longer than the human lifespan although some other life-forms – yew trees for instance, live for several thousand years. It's good to imagine how they see the changes that happen over their long lifetimes.

Each of these points, these moments of change, are determined for us here on Earth by our planet's revolution around the sun, and by the Earth's rotation on her own axis. They are also determined by our sun's movement within our home galaxy, the Milky Way, and further determined by the movement, the dance, of our galaxy within the whole cosmos, for our galaxy moves and dances with all the other galaxies in the universe.

Animals determine when to breed, plants know when to flower and fruit as well as when to die back and lose their leaves through the dance of the Earth with the sun. We humans use these seasons to determine how and when to sow and plant-out our vegetables, when fruit will be ready to harvest, when to move back down the mountain to the warmer valleys from the high summer pastures, even what our weather is likely to be, by the dance our Earth does with the Sun.

We make calendars and almanacs to help us remember this; some of them, like Stonehenge are about 5,000 years old; the Mesolithic arrangement of twelve pits and an arc found in Aberdeenshire, Scotland, is twice as old, dating back to10,000 years ago. The Aberdeenshire calendar has been described as a lunar calendar and is the world's oldest known calendar to date. We've been measuring time for a long time. Calendars are ways of showing us what time we are in. In the miniature timescale of a day, we determine time with clocks; they help us know when to get up, go to work, have a lunch break, come home, catch a train, watch TV, go to bed. And clocks, too, work through where our planet is relative to the sun and the stars.

We count the days, months and years, and give them numbers, so we know how old we are, how long we've been in a relationship, had the car, when the cat's birthday is, when the rent/mortgage gets paid, when we'll retire – all that stuff. And, perhaps, we have an idea that all these numbers have some significance, even if we pooh-pooh it and laugh at ourselves (embarrassedly) when we're with friends and family, or down the pub.

Going In & Coming Out

The spiral of going in and coming out again is central to many traditions including my own British one, it's found in one of the British symbols, the Troytown. The name Troytown comes from the old Welsh/Brythonic words, Caer y Troieau which means city of turns, or turning city. It reminds me of Arianrhod's spinning tower of inspiration; Arianrhod has a strong hand in, and a lot of influence on, the old skills and craft of numbers.

Here's the Troytown labyrinth again.

Figure 41: Troytown

The oldest known form of this labyrinth in Britain is over 4,000 years old and is carved into the rock wall behind a ruined mill next to where my father used to live down in North Cornwall. I've been following its path for most of my life, using it, working with it and allowing it to show you what the numbers can tell you really works.

Put your finger on the entranceway to the Troytown and follow the pathway through to the centre. The journey takes you in and out, round and round, to the centre, the heart of creation *and* of yourself – then you follow the path back out again into the world. Note how the path takes you first in close to the centre then out to the edge, then back in almost to the middle only to go back out again before you turn back and finally arrive at the centre.

Do that, follow the labyrinth in and out. Feel it show you about going into the heart of everything, and then about opening out, expanding to know yourself part of everything.

The two spirals of the labyrinth hold the energies of life, the universe and everything.

Of course, like the labyrinth, you are never going only one way. The more you discover about yourself the more you come to know about the interconnectedness of everything. The two journeys facilitate each other, the inward and outward journeys work and spiral together, like the eastern form we may know better, the Yin Yang.

The idea of in-and-out reminds us of breathing. Everything breathes, it's a cycle-thing. The in-breath draws energy from heaven to earth, involution. The out-breath draws energy from earth to heaven, evolution.

When you know this, you know yourself. As the old Taoist adage says, "*You cannot change anything but yourself. But, in changing yourself you find the world changes around you.*" The path through the numbers takes you inwards, in to your roots, then outwards to relate to the rest of creation.

The Spirit-self as Builder

You, the real you, which continues through many incarnations is your spirit. It returns to the Earth, or another planet, many times in order to learn and grow, expand its knowing and become ever more inclusive. Each incarnation provides the opportunity to learn more and more about the world, the universe and everything.

When the spirit goes into incarnation it needs a spacesuit for whichever planet it has chosen to live on; the one we know best, of course, is Planet Earth as that's where we are now. Your body and your personality, even your name, make up that spacesuit. For instance, the person called Elen Sentier is only the spacesuit I'm wearing for my current incarnation on Earth. The spirit-me is the one who *inhabits* this spacesuit, and currently answers to the name of Elen. The spirit-me isn't always female, I remember several incarnations when I was male; and I've not always had the same sexual orientation either, sometimes I've been gay (either male or female oriented) and I remember an incarnation as transgender too. I know a lot of people who have similar memories but not everyone always comes into incarnation with memories of previous lives, sometimes that doesn't suit our spirit's purpose, sometimes not remembering means we're more likely to have the experiences we need in that lifetime.

How does all this come about?

When I was a child Dad told me the following story ...

'You know the person you are when you go to sleep,' he began, 'the one who goes travelling, like when you go on adventures in the stars?' I nodded. 'Well, that person is your spirit-self.'

'Is that why I know so much more when I'm dreaming?'

Dad grinned, 'Yup,' he said.

'I wish I could remember it all when I'm awake,' I complained.

'One day, you will,' he ruffled my hair. 'Now, let's get on with the story ...

'Before you were born, before Mummy and I even decided we wanted you, your spirit found us and came to talk with us about your next trip to Earth. We all got together, perhaps in a café over there in otherworld but, I think ...' he paused, looking at me, 'I think it was at the Shapeshifters' Arms. That's a really lovely pub in otherworld where we all get together, us and Merlin, and Pan, and all the rest of our Gang. There's lots and lots of us in the Gang and, one day, you'll get to know more of them, probably visit the Shapeshifters' yourself. Anyway, we all got together over a bottle of good wine ... and a wee dram or two,' he grinned again, knowing I knew his penchant for single malts, 'and we discussed your next Earth-trip. That's when we agreed we'd like to be your parents, and you agreed you thought we'd do all the things you needed for the trip. So we agreed on a date when Mummy and I would come together to make the seed of your body-self.

'Now, the next bit was all up to you. There's what I call a

big warehouse over there in otherworld [*Dad was an engineer, so these concepts came naturally to him, he often used them as examples*] where they keep everything anyone could need for making a body-self, a spacesuit for any planet, anywhere in the universe. So you went along and rang the bell on the counter to get the storekeeper's attention. When he came, you said, "I need all the stuff for a spacesuit for Planet Earth, please."

'Well, then he asked you for more specifics so you said you needed some physical matter to make your physical body out of, and some feeling-stuff to make your feelings from, and some thinking-stuff to do your thinking with, and some intuitive-stuff so you'd have some intuition to learn to work with. And that all of these bits must come from the Planet Earth store, from her own body, because if they didn't they wouldn't work there and your whole spacesuit would be rejected, which would be very uncomfortable for your spirit. So the storekeeper went off and came back after a while with four boxes marked, Body, Feelings, Thinking and Intuition, and all marked "gifted by Planet Earth".

'You took them away and then, later, after Mummy and I had made your seed, you jumped in and began putting the whole jolly boiling together. After nine months you knocked on Mummy's womb wanting to be let out, so she birthed you ... and here you are. Didn't so a bad job of that making either!' he chuckled.

Does that help, make some sense? I hope so, it certainly did for me.

Our spirit-self creates the *vessel* – the physical body and personality – in which it can live for the incarnation; and which will also be right for all the stuff it wants to do in that incarnation. That can mean a body that doesn't function as well as it might, perhaps has some diseases and/or accidents. All sorts of things may be part of our spirit's plan for learning, they're certainly not wished on us by some malevolent god!

Our spirit also creates the job-plan which it hopes to achieve this time around.

It needs that *vessel*, spacesuit, to enable it to function on Earth; spirits can neither effect nor affect much in the everyday without the help of a material body to actually interact with the world it's living on. In some traditions this *vessel* is called the *golden cup* or *grail* and it's composed of your personality and your physical body. I really like Dad's name for it ... the spacesuit we wear for getting around on Planet Earth.

Your spirit decides, in concert with your spirit group, which will include your parents-to-be, on the job it wishes to do this time around. The spirit group (we call it tylwyth which means *the folk*, as in tylwyth teg meaning the fair folk) are the friends and relations you've known and worked with for many lifetimes, like I have with my Mum and Dad, and many others too that I've met again in the flesh this lifetime.

Like in Dad's story, your spirit goes to the store and asks the planet if it may *borrow* some planetary matter with which to build its vehicle. The borrowing is important, the stuff must be made from the matter of the planet the spirit is going to live on or, like an organ transplant, it'll get rejected. Dad's story to the eight-year-old me simplified this a bit, but I learned it all in greater depth as I grew up.

So what happens? It's like this, in rough engineering terms ...

To build your *physical/sensing* body, the spirit borrows physical/sensing matter from the planet and builds your physical body out of it.

To build your *feelings/emotional* body, it borrows planetary feeling/emotional matter and builds your feelings body.

To build your *thinking/mental* body, it borrows planetary thinking/mental matter and builds your thinking body.

To build your *intuitive* body, it borrows planetary intuitive matter and builds that too.

The intuitive body is also the recorder for the incarnation, the hard disc on which all your life-experience is recorded; when you die it uploads all your life-experience into the ancestral cauldron. It holds your job-description for this incarnation too.

Then your spirit pours the whole lot into the alchemical flask of your mother's womb, brews it for nine months, sparks it – i.e. jumps in and en-spirits it, at around 3 months gestation. Then, at birth-time, the spirit stirs your mother's womb to begin labour.

End result: *you* – a flesh-covered personality-self containing a spirit who is waiting for the personal-self to get in touch so they can begin to work consciously together.

Your spirit has to wait until your personality-self is sufficiently grown up to be able to communicate with it. It is the personality-self that contacts the spirit, *not* the other way round. The spirit waits for the call, it *cannot* be the first to make contact; the personality-self must open the door … i.e. the little you must choose to be conscious.

Later, at the end of your incarnation, it's your spirit who knows when it's time to pull the plug and bring you to death, usually because you've finished the job. Even if the manner of your death *appears* to be an accident that's rarely the case, it's very likely the accident was intentional (from the point of view of all the spirits caught up in it) so more lessons may be learned by all involved. Things almost never happen only to you, there are always others involved, and their spirit-learning is just as important as yours. What happens to you can equally be of benefit to them. Life and death are inclusive.

At death, your spirit returns the planetary matter it borrowed back to the Earth, hopefully in a *more evolved and inclusive state* than when it borrowed it. This is the major way of doing planetary healing: borrowing planetary matter, living it really well and then handing it back in better shape when you die. That's part of your bargain when you borrow it. If you haven't evolved, grown personally, then the planetary matter Earth loaned your spirit could be in the same, or even in a worse, state than when you borrowed it some three-score-years-and-ten ago.

You can imagine how embarrassed your spirit would feel at having to apologise to the Earth for such an event! Try not to let that happen ...

Spiritual Engineering

In order to work with your numbers it's useful to have a grasp of this process of spiritual engineering, know how your personal-self was constructed, by whom and for what purpose. You may already realise that there are no conscripts to incarnation ... only volunteers!

Think of it this way ...

At first, you're only conscious of your personal-self, so you sit happily in the seat of the personal self and may not realise, for a while, there is another perspective.

Then, as you grow more aware, you realise there is another place to sit, the seat of the spirit, and you explore moving to that place. By changing your seat, you change your perspective, you see things as the spirit does which is a much wider and deeper view than the personal-self has on its own.

But, for each incarnation, you always see through the lens of the personal-self your spirit has created. This not only enables you to speak and be heard in the world – spirits don't usually make much sense to everyday folk without a personality to speak though – but also for the spirit (through the personality) to experience all the things it wanted to for its incarnation. Becoming conscious of, and learning to work with, your spirit-self doesn't mean you lose your personal viewpoint, there would be no point in that. You add to it, make your personal-self large and more inclusive so it can encompass both. The integrated personal-self becomes the lens that focuses for both the spirit and the personal – and that's much closer to 20/20 vision.

At death you return the planetary matter you've worn and used for the incarnation. By refining the material that your spirit borrows you give the matter back in a better state than when you borrowed it – and so heal the planet.

The Integrated Personal-self

The personal-self is made of what in esoteric-speak are called the four subtle bodies, and they're made from planetary matter, the stuff of the subtle bodies of the Earth, our home-planet. They correlate to the four elements earth, water, air and fire, and to Jung's four functions ...

Figure 42: Jung numbers & elements

Numbers	Element	Jung
8-1	Earth	Sensing-physical self
7-2	Water	Feeling self
6-3	Air	Thinking self
5-4	Fire	Instinctive/intuitive self

The personal-self becomes integrated when the four subtle bodies are all aligned and working well together in an *appropriately* balanced way. Note: balance does not always (or even often) mean equally weighted! It's usually more like this picture ...

Figure 43: Balance 3

The simplest way to get to know the subtle bodies is to work with them through Jung's functions; these are the forms we know best and are most in touch with.

Sensation is something most of us are fairly good at. It's about touch, sight, smell, hearing and taste – experiences like hot, cold, pain, pleasure, the bodily sensations through which we know the physical world. It's also about the body and what it knows, we call it body-knowing. The body holds a great deal of knowledge, as well as learned responses to various situations like pulling your hand away from a flame or running like hell if a sabre-toothed tiger is after you. It also knows more subtle things like when people are lying to you, or when they are happy or angry.

Feelings are something we may also be reasonably au fait with, although not everyone is. We all have feelings and emotions and we're reasonably used to them, although some people are more emotionally literate than others. It's an important part of getting to know yourself to learn to be emotionally literate, and your spirit-self needs this just as much as your personality-self does.

Thinking is something we're usually quite proud of, even if we're not actually rocket-science material. We're encouraged to learn to think and reason early on. If we keep at it, we can get quite good at the process of making *logical* connections between things. While this is a useful trait to develop it's very important to remember that the thinking self is only good for some things; it helps us get up in the morning, cook supper, catch the right train, drive the car. But it's not good at *knowing*, that's a different part of the self. The best way to get in touch with it is actually through body-knowing and the sensory self which will lead us to the instincts and intuition.

Instinct &Intuition can be so difficult as we're educated to be rational and use our thinking for all things. We're encouraged to want and need everything to be proved, to believe what's written in books or told us by somebody with alphabet soup after their name. We tend to pooh-pooh our own hunches, as we've been taught to call them, preferring to believe in *coincidence* whilst not realising what that word means.

To be aligned, these four bodies need to be working together in harmony, both with each other *and* with the spiritual and physical realms. Each body needs to function at the right moment, in the right place and in *appropriate*, and often not equal, ways.

Our subtle bodies need to get the hang of being balanced in odd-seeming ways; we need to expand our outlook to understand balance far more deeply. This is how they will best function throughout our lives, and the numbers show us how, for the numbers are about being balanced in the most appropriate way for the moment.

Long ago I got this aphorism ... *what you see depends on what you're looking at and where you're looking from.* It's a good one to keep in mind!

This example might help, and make you laugh ... it's not a lot of good screaming with terror and getting all emotional with a hungry crocodile who is only looking at you as lunch. Instead, turning your thinking on to a high power to find a way out, and making sure your body is running faster than an Olympic sprinter, may get you out of trouble. Unfortunately, for the crocodile, it will also deprive the beastie of its lunch!

In that example, your thinking and physical bodies are the two most needed functions. You can have a good scream with your emotional function later, once your brain and your legs have got you well away to a safe place where you can cry into a cup of tea. As far as your intuitive self is concerned, forget it; it obviously wasn't working well in the first place (or you've not learned to listen to it) which is how you nearly ended up as crocodile-lunch. Sort it out later!

When your subtle bodies are aligned and working properly you'll be able to fit actions appropriately to situations. The surest way of knowing when they are aligned is being able to recognise when you are acting appropriately and when you're not.

Shadow & Duality

Shadow gets a lot of bad press in many new age circles. It seems people are very stuck in exclusive either/or stuff rather than the inclusive and/and, something that needs to change if we're not to get stuck in only knowing what we already know. Everything has a shadow and without this shadow it would have no form, we would not be able to see it. Ursula le Guinn puts this beautifully in LEFT HAND OF DARKNESS. In the novel, the hero and his companion are escaping across a glacier, it takes months for them to do this and, at this point, they find themselves in what's known as a white-out. The hero's description shows us how vital shadow is to enable us to see, know, where we are ... by showing us what is not self and not-self.

> ... Towards the middle of Nimmer, after much wind and bitter cold, we came into a quiet weather for many days. If there was storm it was far south of us, down there, and we inside the blizzard had only an all but windless overcast. At first the over cast was thin, so that the air was vaguely radiant with an even, sourceless sunlight reflected from both clouds and snow, from above and below. Overnight the weather thickened somewhat. All brightness was gone leaving nothing. We stepped out of the tent on to nothing. Sledge and tent were there, Estraven stood beside me, but neither he nor I cast any shadow. There was dull light all around, everywhere. When he walked on the crisp snow no shadow showed the footprint. We left no track. ...

Without shadow the travellers can distinguish nothing, they cannot place themselves in the landscape, they cannot even see the tracks of where they've walked. So it is in life. We *need* shadow to differentiate ourselves from other things, in order to find ourselves and where we are in our lives and relationships with everything. We need duality, self *and* shadow, in order to know ourselves and the world we live in.

In order to work with your numbers, it's necessary to grow yourself into the concept that shadow is an *integral* part of the whole. This doesn't mean that being selfish and mean is acceptable, nor any of the other human traits which don't make for harmonious relationships. But it does mean that the shadow is necessary to enable the whole to even be seen, let alone grow. As human beings, we walk between light and dark, constantly moving between them weaving patterns of life.

Again, Le Guin has another lovely poem in LEFT HAND OF DARKNESS which expresses this ...

> *Light is the left hand of darkness*
> *And darkness the right hand of light.*
> *Two are one, life and death, lying*
> *Together like lovers in kemmer,*
> *Like hands joined together,*
> *Like the end and the way.*

Shadow is the way we know dark/light, goddess/god, womb/phallus, all the pairs of opposites that make up the sacred duality of life, the universe and everything. It's inclusive *and/and* ... not exclusive *either/or*. Life is inclusive.

So shadow is a vital part of the Celtic tradition, and part of Life. Where we live, Middleworld, is the place of shadows, of action, the place where things can happen, where things can change, grow and evolve. Without movement there can be no change, and so no Life. By living, moving and working in Middleworld, we weave the patterns of life, help create the infinite rainbow shadows that are beingness. It's awe-inspiring. Spend a little time pondering on this; allow it to sink into your body-knowing rather than ferreting it about in your thinking-self like a terrier with a bone. It really does change everything.

Another way of looking at the shadow concept is through the story of Peter Pan. This story was written by a theosophist who put the whole allegory together to show many spiritual points. Peter Pan had had his shadow cut off when he was a baby and ran away to play with the Lost Boys. As long as he had no shadow he could never grow up. That is true for all of us. If we refuse (cut off) our shadow then we cannot grow up. We all know old age pensioners who still have the emotional age of a five-year-old, with concomitant irresponsibility. In the story, Peter Pan gets Wendy to sew his shadow back on and so is able to return to the everyday world. He doesn't find this altogether easy or attractive as he quickly becomes accountable and responsible for his actions, painful but it's the only way to become whole.

Being whole is about living an *and/and* life. Most of us somehow find ourselves living exclusive lives, *either/or* lives. We don't naturally include. We need to be able to distinguish between self and other, but we also need to see our connections too.

Think of a coin. It has a head and a tail, two sides but it's one whole coin, made up of both sides it could not be whole without both. This is like us. Humans often struggle with this, it's not how our education and morality systems teach us things are, or should be, so it requires lots of mind-stretching. But mind-stretching is fun.

Ancestors

Ancestors are part of spirit groups. They're not always, or even often, part of our DNA flesh, blood and bone relations. The physical matter is not really crucial to our purposes ... except for the purpose of the current incarnation; the spirit family to which we belong is far more significant. Sometime our ancestors have shared physical family, racial and/or tribal lives with us, but not always. Our spirit-self experiences all races and genders and orientations to complete its knowing of life, so blood relations are a very small part of this. Our true family is our spirit group. As I said above, in the Brythonic language we call this the tylwyth, as in tylwyth teg which means fair folk ... tylwyth means "folk" or people, so our spirit group is our people.

Ancestors hold the cauldron of wisdom – what eastern

traditions call karma or the Akashic records – the ancestors hold the wisdom of everything that has ever happened.

Taliesin, one of our famous British seers, tells us how to connect with this wisdom in his song that begins "I am a stag of seven tines ...". It's a song about *being* everything, he tells how he is everything. One of my early teachers told me this and ended by saying, "Until you have been a worm, been a maggot, a fly, a mountain, a tree, you are not awenydd!" and she was right. Awenydd is a spirit keeper, and to keep spirit you must know it, and to know it you must be it; this is what real shapeshifting is about, sharing consciousness.

The ancestors hold all this for us. This knowing-through-being is very different from knowing through reading and study, or even watching and listening – which are only *knowing about* something. To be, become, share the consciousness of something, you have to trust it, and yourself, and you need to gain its trust. When you both have this trust you can twine-threads as we call it, share consciousness with it. Most humans are control-freaks with regard to allowing themselves to share consciousness with anything else; they say it's impossible because this excuses them from having to try which, in its turn, would mean they have to change their own inner attitudes. Working with the ancestors helps us grow more inclusive so we can allow this ... work with your numbers will help you do this.

Taliesin knows-in-his-bones how it is to be a stag, a wind, or a tear dropped by the sun, and this is what we can learn too. His song is a riddle-poem which is how our ancestors in Britain worked, through riddles and satire, similar to the better-known Zen koans; our riddles (like the koans) are meant to make you think too. You don't just accept things but ponder and work and sit with them, which allows their meaning to seep into you as your personal-self is ready to accept it. As that happens you get an aha-moment, wonderful, glorious, no words to describe that feeling of knowing-in-your bones. Ancestral knowing is like this.

The spirit is what initiated, began and planned, this incarnation which you are living through your current personality, the space-suit for Planet Earth that you're wearing for this lifetime. Your tylwyth, your folk, your people, are with you when you choose to contact them and can be found through the realm of the ancestors. You may already have noticed that you can feel closer to some friends than to blood-family members, now you have an inkling as to why. Blood may be thicker than water but spirit-links are far stronger than blood ties and much older.

Your spirit came into being as part of your tylwyth in what would seem to your personality a very long time ago. Your spirit has incarnated many times, in many places, in any forms (including animal and plant forms) and all genders, races, creeds and political persuasions. In some incarnations you've been quite a nasty person – we all have – while in others you've been relatively nice. Sometimes you've been clever, sometimes intelligent, sometimes dumb, sometimes you've been cruel, sometimes kind. This is how we learn.

Your spirit needs to experience all life-forms, all natures – why? Because all of this goes back into the cauldron at the end of each incarnation and so increases the knowing, the kenning, of the universe, the cosmos, everything. The universe is continuously growing, through us and through all creation – trees, cats, cars, earthquakes, stars, computers and humans – increasing its wisdom from the experiences of everything.

Our spirits are part of this wholeness; we are part of everything, part of the universe, of the cosmic consciousness which is ever-changing and growing, including more and more experience. The ancestors hold the thread of this consciousness and we can contact it through those threads. They wait for our personal selves in each incarnation to choose to contact them when we feel the urge, the itch, to explore what is beyond our little personal world. Full understanding takes lifetimes … if, indeed, that's ever possible with something that is always growing and changing ... but that's not a problem, imagine the adventures that lie before you in future lifetimes. Exciting!

Bringing it to Light

Your numbers bring all this to light within you so you can see, know, understand and internalise it all and realise your true self. As you come to know yourself you're better able to do your spirit-work. This is the most satisfying thing in the world.

This has massive advantages:

You no longer fear death. You know, absolutely, that you have incarnated in many bodies and that you will do so many times again.

You know you are never alone. You remember how it has been before. You know you have friends and work-mates who are not presently incarnate but who you can converse with them across the worlds. And that they can help you.

If you fear neither death nor loneliness you are less likely to be selfish. In consequence you won't start wars (street-size or country-size) or be cruel to anything that doesn't seem to be like yourself; you can work with difference.

You won't work in competition with other people, so all the ills of advertising, normality, one-up-man-ship, scoring, peer pressure, et al, won't exist for you. If these cease to exist for enough people then whole industries which contribute to harming the planet will die of neglect.

Becoming whole helps the whole planet and everything that lives and breathes and has its being thereon.

Working with your Numbers

Birth Number

Your birth number is the number which all the figures in your date of birth-date reduce down to. The birth number is the "job description" you worked out with your tylwyth spirit group for your current incarnation. The next chapter has some examples for you to work with to help show you how to explore your job for this lifetime.

Like in ordinary, everyday jobs, in order to do them well you need to come to a real understanding of just what it is you signed on for; you need the job description your birth number gives you, so you can learn to work it out.

Learning to understand your birth number can take time and you'll probably be looking at it and reworking it for years, always be seeing new bits, extras, and getting new insights as your own understanding grows. It's rather like watching a really good film, or reading an excellent book, each time you read or see it you get a little bit more, see something new, get a new angle on it. Your life is rather like Doctor Who's spaceship, the Tardis, it's much bigger on the inside than it may appear from the outside; it's also an excellent story, well worth reading and exploring. The numbers offer you ways to do this.

Numerology Calculations: calculating your numbers with this system is very simple and, like most numerology systems, is one of reduction – i.e. 23 = 2+3 = 5

Your birth number is composed of ...

DAY – relationship of the planetary rotation to the sun
MONTH – relationship of Earth to Sun
YEAR – relationship of the Earth to the solar system
CENTURY – relationship of the Earth to the Universe

Your birth number was arranged and calculated by you-the-spirit in concert with your spirit-group/clan, tylwyth, before you were conceived. You can't change this number – so you organise your other numbers to work with it, in support of your job for this lifetime.

Name Choices

Our birth number is something we can't change but we have complete control over our name number, once we reach adult age, and can change it however and whenever we wish. We don't have to stay with any of the names our parents gave us, or any names we acquire through marriage, unless we choose to. Our name number is under our own control. Depending on how aligned our personal-self is with our spirit-self we can choose to align our name number so the two work well together, and it aids with our spirit-job.

If you ask your spirit-self and your allies to help you choose what name to use in order to be best able to fulfil the job you incarnated for this time around you'll really strengthen your abilities. Part of this choosing and asking could be to find out if it would be useful to add in any numbers that may be missing from your birth numbers; always ask, sometimes it really isn't a good idea to add them in. Go back and ponder on what I said about empty space and leaving room, space, for creative new things to come in. Not having a particular number in your chart gives you this space. Don't feel that you absolutely must fill those spaces.

Name Numbers & the Personal Self

Name numbers define the outline and potential of your personal-self in the current lifetime in the light of the spirit's purpose. Birth numbers are the blueprint for the home, the grail-cup, which the spirit can inhabit in the current lifetime. The name number can be likened to the facilities of that home, the washing machine, computer, car, mobile phone, the furniture and decoration. All the things which help your spirit to have a fruitful incarnation. If your name numbers don't enhance your birth number, perhaps even work against it, then it's like living in an inconvenient house with all the wrong facilities, furniture and decoration for the life you lead. You can change your name. With care, inspiration and lots of asking your spirit-self and you tylwyth, you can find a name which brings out and/or adds to the qualities your spirit needs to do its job in the current incarnation.

How do you do this?

We discussed earlier how the spirit decides on an incarnation and the job it wants to do in it, in concert with its spirit-group. Most of us, on getting born are hit with a bad case of spiritual amnesia, we haven't a clue why we decided to come down this time. For a while, this is usually a good thing. If we knew what the whole plan was before our personalities are strong enough to hold that knowledge we would run out on the job. It would be too big, too much, and too in our face. The spiritual amnesia allows the personal-self space and time to grow without knowing the full size and scale of the job, which would be a knockout. Also, knowing the job would change the choices we make in our lives, we would try not to make mistakes ... and those mistakes might well be vital to our learning!

However, there comes a time when we, the personal-self self, can choose to wake up and smell the coffee. We often read avidly at this time and may well become 'course junkies', but the work that works best is what we do ourselves. Other people's ideas and experiences are very useful, we can fill our Cauldron of Knowledge with them, but we need to cook them into a suitable form for our own personal digestive system. And then we must learn to eat slowly, savouring each mouthful, chewing it properly, not gorging and allowing it to digest before we pack more in. All of these are difficult things to master.

We can learn to work directly with our own spirit, our first master, the one who really does know why we're here. There's an old adage, 'You get more sense talking to the engineer than you do to the greasy rag!' Our spirit is the engineer, everyone else is (in the nicest possible way) the greasy rag. It's not that they're stupid or malicious but the cannot know our spirit's purpose for us, not even if they're the best clairvoyant in the whole world.

For how to do this, go to the next chapter and read the piece on Contacting Your Spirit.

Name Number

Each letter of the alphabet is given a number, very simply, as below.

1	2	3	4	5	6	7	8	9
A	B	C	D	E	F	G	H	I
J	K	L	M	N	O	P	Q	R
S	T	U	V	W	X	Y	Z	

Figure 44: alphabet numbers

You write out the names, put the numbers for each letter underneath and add them, reducing down to a single number for each name. You then add these name numbers together and reduce them down to a single figure for the final name number.

You should take the name that you like to be known by and spell it that way. This is who you have chosen to be at this time. For interest later you can take the whole gamut of names your parents might have loaded you with and see what they come out to. This can change your mind about what you call yourself.

Name Number

Your name number is made from the names your parents gave you and/or the names you've chosen for yourself during the lifetime, including names you may take on through partnerships as well as choices in how you want to be called at any time. It works in conjunction with your birth number but is, as you can see, much more flexible.

Each letter of the alphabet is given a number, they're very simple, as below ...

You write out the names, put the numbers for each letter underneath then add them, reducing down to a single number for each name. You then add these name numbers together and reduce them down to a single figure for the final name number.

When working this out you should take the name that you like to be known by and spell it that way. This is your choice, who you've chosen to be at this time. For interest later you can take the whole gamut of names your parents might have loaded you with and see what they come out to. This may change your mind about what you call yourself as well as show you how some of the paths you've trodden to get to today have come about.

Vowels have an extra significance, we'll go into this in the examples in the next chapter.

Birth, Name & Conception

Knowing and working with your numbers is fun but it's also quite complex. It's all about and/and, you're not only your birth number, you're also your name number, and your conception number is important too. Each contains so much, and *all* of it is useful.

Birth Number: your birth number is unchangeable. It is the innate, underlying Power, chosen by your spirit before conception.

Name Number: your name number is the adjustable factor which you can shape and tune to best use the birth-power your spirit built into you at incarnation.

Conception Number: your conception number is the other unchangeable factor. It adds further depth to you birth number and deepens your knowing about your job.

Most people don't know when they were conceived but, occasionally, some do. If you or a friend is a reliable dowser you can find out this way; the best question-system to use is along these lines ...

Firstly, make a guess at when you were conceived simply by going back nine months. Add a week either side and ask ...

1. Was I conceived between X and Y? [give the dates you've reckoned]
   a. If you get a YES go to 2 below, *otherwise* ask, "Was I conceived before X?"
   b. If you get a YES make another two-week period back from that date and ask the question at 1 again.
   c. If you get NO ask ... Was I conceived after Y?
   d. If you get a YES here (which you should do if you've had no up to now) make a two-week period forward from Y and ask the question at 1 again.

You should now have arrived where you can go to 2

2. For the days between X and Y, list each day individually. Put your finger on the first date and ask "Was I conceived on [say the date, including the month and year]?" If you get NO go to the next date and continue until you get YES.

Incidentally, if you want an astrological chart for your conception you can use the same technique to find the date, and adapt it slightly to find the time.

If, when dowsing, you get unclear answers this is because you are being unclear in your questions; you probably have too much emotional investment in the question. Stop. Wait until your emotional need has worn off before you dowse again.

Working with your Numbers

The best way to get the hang of this is to go through the examples in the next chapter. Following those through will show you how to do it ... and then you'll feel really confident to have a go at your own.

Numbers Grid

The numbers grid is a way of recording the numbers in both your birth number and your name number so you can easily see what numbers you have, and how many of each. The numbers grid looks like this ...

$$
\begin{array}{c}
0 \\
9 \\
8 - 1 \\
7 - 2 \\
6 - 3 \\
5 - 4
\end{array}
$$

Figure 45: numbers grid

To use the numbers grid you write out the birth number, say it's 20 12 1944

Then you put the 2 of 20 beside the 2 in the grid; the 0 beside the 0; the 1 beside the 1; the next 2 beside the other 2; the next 1 beside the other 1; the 9 beside the 9; and the two 4s beside the 4.

Your grid will look like this table ...

$$
\begin{array}{lll}
0 & 0 & \\
9 & 9 & \\
8 & 1 & 11^2 \\
7 & 2 & 22 \\
6 & 3 & \\
5 & 4 & 44^2
\end{array}
$$

Figure 46: Table 1

This grid shows you several things straight away: this person has no 8s, 7s, 6s, 5s or 3s; and they have three numbers in pairs; and they have one 9 and one zero.

Remembering the numbers 8, 7, 6, and 5 are on the spirit-side, you can see straight away that this person – in their original agreement for this incarnation – has given themselves lots of space to play and learn about spirit while, at the same time, they've also given themselves lots to play with on the personal side.

They have neither 6 nor 3 so, they've left themselves lots of room here to learn about both sides of the wisdom/intellect pair.

They have three pairs of numbers; this means their intention with each of these pairs is to work with them through the lens of 2-ness, the feeling-self. With the number 1 they learn about the physical body, sensing and the Earth through their feelings; similarly, they intend to learn about both love and the emotions through their feelings, which is likely to be quite intense. They also intend to learn about their instincts and intuitive selves through their feelings. Woof! That sounds like a heavy job to me, to learn and grow everything through the feelings, especially as they've not given themselves any hooks into wisdom and intellect.

They've given themselves both a zero and a 9, so they have lots of contact with the void, the sun, chaos and eternity, and with mirroring! Like I said, Woof! A big job, very worth doing but also very hard work.

So you see, using the numbers grid gives you lots of information very quickly once you come to understand them. It gives you the spread, like a hand of cards.

When you work with your own numbers you may find that you have none of one or two numbers as this person did – all the examples in the next chapter lack some – but this doesn't mean you're a deformed person spiritually it's about leaving space as well as giving yourself tools. Remember, you came in to do a job, like the person in the example above. You arranged your birthday, with the help of your friends in your tylwyth, so you'd have a particular set of number-tools to give you access to the qualities you need to do *this* job, and the space to acquire new ones.

Sometimes the lack of a particular tool can be just what you need to spark you in creative ways – like you don't have a screwdriver so you "manage" by using a knife blade. Your lack of a particular number can encourage you to find new ways of doing that number, as this person is doing through having three pairs. This is a very indirect and subtle way to do things which will require them to work hard, and explore a lot, through their feeling self. Additionally, giving yourself space through lacking a number allows there to be room for new ideas to come through, like that blank canvas.

Once they know they have no 3 or 6 in their numbers they can begin to discover how to bring the qualities of those numbers into their lives. There's more than one way of doing this. They've given themselves a lead through having three pairs; they may also choose to change their name; they could find it works through changing their job, or job-title; perhaps even a relationship change might help. They have space to grow.

They may also find having the gap, the lack of a number, gives them more insight to help others who lack numbers be creative in their ways forwards too. They may find themselves in sympathy with people in the same boat, who also lack numbers, even if those numbers they lack are different.

A space is often a waiting place, it may be waiting for you to find out what it is and what it does. And you know now to do this by asking the number to show you about itself and the space it's left for you to explore.

Dates

Let's look further into how these numbers work.

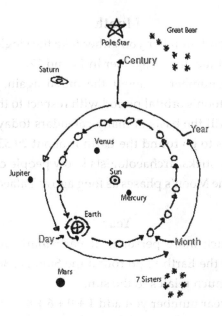

Figure 47: day month year century

When we work with our numbers we take all these factors into account – the day, month, year and century, and all of the appear in our date of birth.

Day – 20
Month – 12
Year – 1968

Let's look at each component ...

Day

The day is the period the earth takes to rotate once on its axis. It relates to both the sun and the moon. To get your day number you either take the single digit, from 1-9, or you add the digits together as in the numbers 11 to 31.

Month

To get your month number you either take the single digit, from 1-9, or you add the digits together in 11 and 12.

The month number is about the moon again. Months are based on the Moon's orbital period with respect to the Earth-Sun line, and are still the basis of many calendars today, the period the Moon takes to go round the Earth is about 29.53 days. From excavated tally sticks, archaeologists know people counted days in relation to the Moon's phases as long ago as Palaeolithic times.

Year

The day is much more personal. It particularly relates to the period it takes the Earth to go round the Sun, i.e. 365.4 days, so the year very much relates to the sun.

To get the year number you add $1 + 9 + 6 + 8 = 24$ so $2+4 = 6$

Each revolution of the Earth around the Sun (year) is significant; it shows you when you came in on the planetary cycle and helps you know where you are in your own cycle.

You've probably noticed that you don't always, or even usually, begin your incarnation cycle with a birthday which adds to 1 ... else we would all be number 1s – a dreadful thought! Neither our own spirits, nor the Earth, nor the universe, would be able to evolve and change if we all had the same number-resonance.

Each year holds and carries its own energy ... and adds its unique flavour to the person's birth number.

Century

This is another way of adding the year and offers you extra numbers to help you understand yourself better.

To get the century number you add $19 + 68$ which give you 87.

This is the addition of the century-number, i.e. 19th century, with the number of years into that century, i.e. 68. It gives the generation flavour to the numbers interpretation.

Each of these numbers for the century reduce to 6 ... but you do *not* reduce the century number down to the 6; there's no need, you already have the reduction to 6 for the year, you don't need it twice. You leave the century number as 87.

The energy of a century covers four generations of human life. Twenty-five years is the average for one generation, meaning the time from when you were born to when you are likely to have your own child. Four generations is –

Child   Parent   Grand-parent   Great-grand-parent

It is just possible for the great-grand-parent to see their great-grand-child. That's the greatest spread of offspring most of us would ever see, or the physical ancestors we could know personally if we take the child's point of view.

As the Planet has her hundred-year anniversary a change happens for her. With each passing century the Earth goes through 1-ness, 2-ness, 3-ness etc. on a much bigger scale than we are able to know with our short lifetimes. When we reduce the century numbers down by adding them together we get ...

1000 = 1+0 = 1 so 1-ness

1100 = 1+1 = 2 so 2-ness

1200 = 1+2 = 3 so 3-ness

And so on to 1900 = 1+9 = 10 = 1 back to 1-ness again

2000 = 2+0 = 2-ness for the century we're currently living in.

If you look at the changes and new beginnings which happened between 1900 and 1999 the sheer number is amazing. Additionally, there was a tremendous population explosion of human beings. In 1900 there were just over 1 billion of us on the Earth, in 1999 there were six billion; that's 6-times as many people in just 100 years! This made a massive difference for those of us born during this period; it altered the way we perceive things from the way our immediate ancestors did; it made huge social changes, and (hopefully) increased awareness of the effects humans have on the planet. So, the century number 19 was very much about newness and change which is a major trait of the number 1 – which 19 reduces down to.

Look at the attributes of each century-number and see how each century expresses those attributes. The century 1800-1899 has the attributes of 9; this was the time of the Industrial Revolution.

From 1700-1799 you are looking at 8 and the Age of Enlightenment.

If you read up about the history of each of those times, and compare this to the number-qualities, it's illuminating.

The century-year sets the tone for that century ... 1900 = 1-ness, 1800 = 9-ness, 1700 = 8-ness, and so on.

Then, every ten years, there's a sub-set of energy ... 2000 = 2-ness, 2010 = 3-ness, 2020 = 4-ness, and so on.

So all the people born between 2000 and 2009 share a 2-ness of decade; those born between 2010 and 2019 share a 3-ness; but it goes further than that. The events in our lives which happen during those periods all share that number quality too.

Examples

The examples in this chapter will help you get the hang of what the numbers mean and how to work with them.

Here are examples of two different people's numbers. I've laid them out just as I would when working with the person. Walk through them slowly, over a cup of tea, allowing them to slowly percolate into your consciousness. Pause when you come across things you don't understand, go through them slowly, maybe go back to a relevant chapter in the book to go over the basics again. If it's really not making sense then put the whole jolly boiling down and go do something else; giving your brain a break always helps, and the break means your thinking-cauldron goes onto the back burner so it brews better. When you come to look at it again you'll likely find more things have slotted into place. This is the best way to work with anything, don't overthink it, don't keep worrying at it like that terrier with a bone, allow it time to work with you, and allow time for your own understanding to take hold of it. Give it and yourself space-time ...

Example – Anny Wyse:
Anny's Birth Numbers
Anny Wyse's birthday is 6.8.1948

Day	Month	Year	Century
6	8	1948	(19+48)
	(6+8)	(1+9+4+8)	67
	14	22	
	(1+4)	(2+2)	
	5	4	
	9		

Figure 48:Anny birth table

You'll see I've added the year number in two different ways, first for the year and second for the century. You use the numbers 1, 9, 4, 8, only once in the numbers grid below, hence I put them in brackets for the century number above. Anny Wyse's birth numbers on the grid look like this.

	0		
^{4}9999	9		
^{5}88888	8	1	1111111^7
^{2}77	7	2	22^2
6	6	3	-
^{5}55555	5	4	444^3

Figure 49: Anny birth grid

You see that Anny has no zeros, two 9s, two 8s, one 7, two 6s, one 5, three 4s, no 3s, two 2s, and two 1s. I've shown the multiples of a number by putting a superscript ^{2} or ^{3} beside them … i.e. Anny has 9 to the power of 2, 8 to the power of 2, 6 to the power of 2, 1 to the power of 2, 2 to the power of 2 and 4 to the power of 3.

Having two ones, one to the power of two, is different from just adding the ones together. It isn't the same as compound numbers either; a compound number, like 11, is a number in its own right. The power of 1-ness in Anny's case is tinted with the power of 2; she does her 1-ness with a 2 flavour.

If you get more than one of any number it, or they, will be your secondary driver(s) after to the number in your birth grid. In this case, Anny has four numbers to the power of 2 and one to the power of 3, so her secondary drivers are 2 and 3.

Anny's birth number is 9. This means her natural tendencies go towards the positive and negative qualities of the void so she will be a powerful person who needs to learn to use her power appropriately; and she will suffer all the temptations of 9-ness ...

Being Invisible – both liking this and wanting to hide, and disliking it because she feels unseen, not heard, and unappreciated.

The Communicator – wanting to communicate with everyone and everything; being angry/upset when she's misunderstood.

The Trickster – enjoying puns; seeking connections others don't see; enjoying riddles and probably poetry; leading people up the garden path; pranks; being slippery and like quicksilver.

Truth – knowing and seeing things easily and clearly; not understanding when others don't; hating hypocrisy and wanting to steamroller those who practise it.

Anny should not try to do anything which requires "politics". Oh, she can see the political ways and means but it would choke her to practise them. If her power is focused on the good of everything rather than personal power, and this is very likely because of the rest of her numbers, she will have no patience whatsoever with people who are selfish, out for themselves, and have no wider or inclusive vision of the planet and humanity as a whole. She will probably despise politicians.

Anny has lots of numbers to the power of 2, these are 9, 8, 6, 2 and 1. This means she will use the energy of these numbers with a flavour of 2-ness, through the feelings lens, and that will be one of her saving graces as well as a challenge some of the time. 9 is not an easy number to be saddled with and, as you'll see, it is also her name number so she has 9-ness very strongly which could easily lead her into being a black hole.

It is extremely hard to encompass the chaotic and evolutionary powers of the void within the human personal self. Anny's spirit self and her spirit-group, her tylwyth, have added the leavening of the feelings self to the difficult broth of her birth number to help her find her way, and her feelings-self is able to add in some humanity. The number 9 is an aspect of both the god of the underworld and the ancestors which, as we shall see, is very useful to Anny but it's not an easy burden.

Human beings are not gods, nor are they meant to be. Gods are difficult to see, they always seem to be clouded in a bright darkness which fools our eyes, or is so dazzlingly bright it blinds us. Fortunately, Anny's strong 2-ness flavour will help her to see into the bright darkness.

In her birth numbers Anny has two 2s. This jumps the power of her feeling self by a couple of orders of magnitude over the base rate which is a big step up. She has to be careful not to go overboard with the feelings.

To recap so far ...

Anny's birth number is 9, a deep and potentially difficult one.

She has 2, the feelings-self, strongly through her secondary drivers as well as having 2 to the power of 2.

She does five out of the eight different numbers in her birth chart to the power of 2, i.e. with a feelings-self flavour.

What else? Anny has 4 to the power of 3, so she tends to work her instinctual self through the lens of thinking-self, and her instincts are up three orders of magnitude over the basic rate which is strong.

Anny's main qualities are ...

Power – which she can use to enable. And this Power is qualified by the feeling self.

A very strong instinctual nature (4), qualified by the lens of her thinking self (3); this gives her the ability to understand her instincts and to question them accurately.

The strong instincts can also give Anny a powerful ability to understand animals, plants and the natural world. To those not blessed with this talent she could seem quite fae and omniscient. This ability to understand brings with it the ability to perceive the pain of the natural world when humans use it unthinkingly or cruelly. When Anny sees this she will likely go ballistic, and might find herself in deep trouble. It's unlikely the trouble will matter to her though as she will care far more about the wrongs to the natural world than for herself.

Additionally, Anny's dislike of hypocrisy, combined with the strong instinctual qualities focused through the mind, means she can see straight through political and humanistic arguments put up to justify cruelty. If I was advising her, I would suggest she avoids any job in which politics, and political correctness are important as although she could do the work, and very well, she'd never survive the politics and might well slaughter her colleagues and bosses, verbally if not physically.

Let's go through her birth numbers ...

1-ness: Anny's two 1s give her a strong grounding ability and a fairly strong personality which she works through her feeling self. She is able to both *sense* and *feel* things well. She will also love her body and want to use it, possibly in dance, sports, something physical and powerful.

2-ness: With two 2s, and using 2 as the focus for most of her other numbers, Anny has a very strong connection with her feelings self. She has the ability to be both empathic and sympathetic, but the underlying 9-ness means she won't suffer stupidity or fools; consequently she will want to point up errors in understanding quite ruthlessly. Not everyone will want to see that. There are two main hazards here, either caring too much or caring too little. The feeling lens has its drawbacks, as do all lenses. Anny must learn to stand back from things, take deep breaths, count backwards to a hundred, anything to keep a real perspective on the events she's working with.

3-ness: Anny has no 3s in her birth number so her thinking-function is hidden and comes out through her instincts, for which it is the focus.

4-ness: Her instinctual function is very strong and this is how Anny does her thinking. She sees the answer, then works backwards to find the process of how to get there; and she does the process-finding work largely so she can explain what she sees to others, certainly not to convince herself. She thinks instinctively rather than wading along in a linear-logical-path fashion. This can be quite incomprehensible to those who don't work this way, so there will likely be plenty of people who cannot understand and may get quite cross with her at times. I doubt this will worry her much.

5-ness: Her single 5 gives her the ability to be in touch with her intuitive body, and use it effectively. As the 5 is focused through the 1, the body-sensing-lens, she will use that body-sensing as the way she works with her intuition. It will also help her stay grounded whilst working intuitively; she should be able to walk between worlds well.

6-ness: The two 6s give Anny a strong knowing ability, qualified by the feeling lens, and this will be a formidable tool for her. She *knows* things, in her bones, and is able to give that knowing the warmth of the feeling self, so making it much more easily understandable to her listeners.

7-ness: The single 7 gives Anny the love-wisdom touch, and this (along with those deep breaths) will help her hold the perspective on her feeling nature. Having just the one 7 means that she, again, uses it through the sensory-body-lens which is both a good grounding force and links it to the way she uses her intuition. Anny will be able to sense things deeply, sense the love-wisdom in things and people, and feel them in her bones; this will help her find ways to act and speak appropriately and so calm down some of her impatience with those who tread a linear path.

8-ness: Anny has a strong connection with Spirit and this likely includes vivid and accurate past-life memories which, again, she works through her feelings lens. She will likely visit the ancestral realms often and be well able to bring back wisdom from there. Combining this with her intuitive and instinctual abilities will be very useful and effective. She must keep her feelings lens clean and bright or she will get into trouble because a clouded feeling lens causes distortion.

9-ness: The two 9s give Anny a very strong connection to the void, the power behind all things, and this too is focused through the feelings lens. It can be a difficult one to handle but will likely attract her more than anything else.

The void both attracts and repels but, to someone with a strong, intelligent instinctual and intuitive nature, along with a good connection to spirit and the ancestral realms, and good ability in *knowing*, the attraction of the void will be far stronger than its repulsion. Anny's instincts, focused through the thinking lens will help her feel quite at home with the energy of the void, unafraid of chaos and very willing to learn to understand it. Whether she can ever put this understanding across to others will be a much harder job, but I expect she'll try.

Anny has no 3s so her thinking self is hidden and she goes at thinking via her instinctual self. If she can line this up with her knowing qualities as expressed by the two 6s, worked through the feelings, she'll be a very good communicator, maybe even abe to get over some of the concepts of the void to others. But this way of thinking probably means she had a hard time at school, and was unlikely to ever have been brilliant at exams or as a scholar, because she just does not, and cannot, come at things from a logical and academic point of view. This won't matter to her though as she finds that sort of thinking far to slow and restrictive, and that again won't go down well with academic-style folk.

Having no zeros means she won't be a scintillating mirror to everyone she meets, and this is a good thing; she could easily scorch everyone around her if she had mirror qualities too.

9 is Anny's number and it will be all the qualities of the 9 which inspirit her life. These qualities are largely focused through her feelings-lens. Both instinct and intuition will be her other strong attribute. Her power is focused through her feeling self and this will be the heart of her life. Her 9-ness will bring out her trickster-self and there will always be an acerbic quality,

an edge to her humour, and a delight in the ridiculous, which comes from the chaos qualities of the 9. Anny will not suffer fools gladly.

An interesting birth chart; now, as we do her name, you'll see how this adds extra power, and difficulties, for Anny.

Anny's Name Numbers

A	N	N	Y	W	Y	S	E
1	5	5	7	5	7	1	5

Figure 50: Anny name

Anny ... 1+5+5+7 = 18 = 9   Wyse ... 5+7+1+5 = 18 = 9

Anny Wyse's name number is also 9, very emphatically so in fact as each name itself adds down to 9, *and* the numbers which make each name are exactly the same although in a different order. This emphasises the numbers even more.

I've put Anny's name number grid beside her birth grid so you can see them together, and see how she has added numbers through her name to give herself more options to fulfil her life-job for her current incarnation.

	Birth				Name		
	0					0	
^{2}99	9				^{2}99	9	
^{2}88	8	1	1111^4		^{2}88	8	1	11^2
^{2}77	7	2				7	7	2	22^2
	6	3			^{2}66	6	3	
^{4}5555	5	4			5	5	4	444^3

Figure 51: Anny birth & name grids

Now we put her birth numbers and her name numbers into the one grid to get a full picture of Anny.

$$0$$
$$^{4}9999 \quad 9$$
$$^{4}8888 \quad 8 \quad 1 \quad 111111^{6}$$
$$^{3}777 \quad 7 \quad 2 \quad 22^{2}$$
$$^{2}66 \quad 6 \quad 3$$
$$^{5}55555 \quad 5 \quad 4 \quad 444^{3}$$

Figure 52: Anny birth + name grid

Looking at Anny's birth and name numbers together gives us a string and clear picture of her. She adds no new numbers from her name to those already in her birth chart but she strengthens all the rest and changes the way she works with them.

Her drivers – the "power of" numbers – are now 6 (knowing, like knowing in your bones), 5 (intuition), 4 (instincts), 3 (thinking), and 2 (feelings); so she's changed the way she works by choosing the name she has.

She still has no zeros or 3s, I suspect her spirit self feels she will do better without the zero as I said above; and she now has two indirect ways of working with her thinking self through the drivers of both her instincts (4) and her love-wisdom connection (7).

She highlights in her name the qualities she feels will best enhance her raison d'etre, her job for this incarnation.

1-ness: She's added four extra 1s, she now has six 1s, a big strengthening of her personal self which she probably feels she needs for what she wants to do in this lifetime. It's possible things like bad experiences at school, not being understood because of the weird instinctual way she thinks, may well have prompted the need to strengthen her personality so she doesn't get wiped out when people criticise her.

She's increased 1-ness to the power of 6 (knowing) and this will really help; she will come to know in her bones when she's right, regardless of what others say or how much alphabet-soup they have after their names.

All those 1s increase her body-knowing and sensing abilities too, and her grounding, so she will hold her own, hold onto her own opinions when these feel appropriate for her rather than giving way to "majority opinion". That can also be a potential danger; she needs to check in with her instincts that this is not an occasion when she needs to change her ways! Both her instincts and her strengthened intuitive ability will be her best guides here.

2-ness: she retains her two 2s with all their strengths, and the 2-ness flavour of the 6, so she still has the empathy she will need to fid her way through the usual tangles of modern life and relationships. She keeps the strong connection between feeling and knowing which is such an invaluable one.

3-ness: while she still has no 3s in her chart she now has both instinct (4) and love-wisdom (7) to the power of 3; she uses her thinking abilities to get a good handle on both these qualities. Now having 7 to the power of 3 really increases her skill in both working with love-wisdom and with making it comprehensible to others.

4-ness: those instincts are still there, and will work for her as I said in her birth numbers. Instinct is an excellent and much underrated quality, perhaps Anny will be able to show others just how useful it is.

5-ness: she's really gone to town here, she now has 5 to the power of 5. Remember what I said about bringing a number up to the power of itself, this means that quality is exceptionally strong in Anny now, her intuition will be working full blast and will be very accurate. Intuition works with instinct, the two go together and are really the way to know the world, the universe and everything.

There are so many links and threads which physicists are now discovering – gravity waves, string theory, pulsars, etc – which can also be felt and known through what we call spirit. Good scientists discover things and then work backwards -as Anny does but maybe at even deeper levels – to find the mechanism for their discovery; one of the famous ones for this is Kekulé who dreamed of snakes in a ring, biting their tails, and came up with the benzine atom. There is also Poincare who saw his equations in clouds. And of course there's Einstein's thought experiments.

6-ness: Anny keeps her two 6s, and she adds the six 1s into the mix too. 6-ness, that knowing in your bones thing, is such an important part of everything, and it's often written off as imagination. It isn't, it's about knowing in ways your frontal cortex can't manage, isn't built to do. Maybe by knowing 6-ness through her body Anny will find ways to transmit this knowing, with conviction, in ways that others can latch onto.

7-ness: Anny now uses the feeling lens to work with her connection to love-wisdom. It's a good way to do this because most people believe they have some handle on what feelings are, and indeed they do.

8-ness: Anny now has 8 to the power of 4, she's turned to her instinctual self as te driver for working with the spirit realm and the ancestors. This is a really good idea. Spirit and the ancestors don't work on the ordinary human intellectual level so doing this connection through the instincts is really going to help Anny. It will also help her confidence in being sure she has the information she learns from the ancestors right; she won't need to try and *think* it – never a good idea anyway.

9-ness: Anny now has four 9s; she came in with two in her birth numbers but her name adds in another two. Again, she's using her instincts to work with the void and that's a very good way of doing it. The thought of the void is weird, strange and perhaps terrifying to many because you just cannot think about it logically. It's a vacuum, an emptiness and an openness too. These ideas bring up thoughts of unsolidity, futility meaninglessness pointlessness, and sometimes even falseness and futility, in many folk, so to actually work with all of this is seriously scary. For Anny, it isn't. For her, it opens up all the possibilities she can imagine and all those she can't imagine too, and that's good. She wants new, she enjoys change, she loves growing, so the void offers her all this. Going at it through her instincts she completely bypasses her linear thinking self and is able to look at all the possibilities three dimensionally. She has opened up a whole other universe for herself with these four 9s.

Anny's name focuses her power. She's a strong person who knows where she's going and has tooled-up, through her name, to make sure she gets there. Likely she will be a loner and quite difficult to live with. She's unlikely to be a feminine woman, and although she's very attractive she probably frightens men off too … well it's quite a challenge living on the edge of a black hole!

The attraction is that, when you actually look, the black hole is not empty but full of beautiful and incredible things. The drawback to anyone attempting to live with her will be keeping your balance on the edge and not being sucked in. Anny wouldn't thank you for diving into her maelstrom and losing yourself in her. She'd be bored to tears by you then, and feel she'd lost a friend. If she was in a dark mood – and all those 9s can help to bring these on when things are not going well – she would feel you had betrayed her by losing yourself in her.

There is a poem in the Celtic tradition from a great bard, Taliesin. It ends …

I am the womb of every holt
I am the blaze on every hill
I am the queen of every hive
I am the shield for every head
I am the tomb of every hope

I feel this poem expresses Anny. It's a weird, shadowy verse, like most Celtic poetry, but it hints strongly at the ability to *be* everything, and this is something Anny is able and willing to do. You see it especially in the body-sensing ability she has given herself with all those ones along with the further enhancement of her instincts and intuition, through which she can work this being-everything stuff. It's a shapeshifter quality which enables those who have it to experience how it is to be something other than themselves – how to be a tree, a mountain, a wildcat or wolf, a fish, a bird, a blade of grass or tiny insect – without losing their own identity. Anny has this quality in spades.

Like all strong personalities, Anny will have to watch out she doesn't shock or trample people out of wanting to hear her; and must also beware of the power of charisma. While charisma can assist your audience in helping people to hear you, you also have to be careful not cast a spell over them, not to enchant them in a 'power-over' manner. That's never a good idea and it will always come back on you if you try it.

I feel Anny will be, already is, a strong communicator, especially of off-the-wall ideas that later prove to be very apt, so the charisma can help that. Using charisma is like walking a tightrope, it requires delicate balance and continual sensing of what is going on, not letting your audience lose themselves in you but keeping them on the point of what you're saying. If she used charisma wrongly it would be easy for Anny to allow herself to become a guru, allow people could put her on a pedestal. Like all of us, she needs to remember the only way off a pedestal is down.

Example 2 – Joanne Donne

Joanne is another fascinating person, with enormous potential and ability, if she will learn to use it, to realise that potential. In my years doing numerology on of the things which has been born in on me is that all people are fascinating ... if only we will look and see them properly.

Joanne was born on 21-11-1981

21	11	1981
(2+1)	(1+1)	(1+9+8+1)
3	2	19
(3+2)		(1+9)
5		10
		(1+0)
		1

(5+1)

6

Figure 53: Joanne birth numbers

Joanne's century number is (19+81) 1 0 0 and her birth numbers grid looks like this ...

^{3}000	0		
^{2}99	9		
8 8	1	111111111^9	
7	2	22^2	
6 6	3	3	
5 5	4		

Figure 54: Joanne birth grid

The first thing which hits you in the eye is the quantity of 1s Joanne has, 1 to the power of 9 in fact. Although her birth number is 6, her focal point, it will be this large number of 1s which will dominate much of the way Joanne does things.

Joanne's nine 1s ensure her sense of her experience of her body will be very strong, as will be her sense of her personal self, her ego and this latter could cause all sorts of problems. Her sensory abilities will be very marked along with her consciousness of physical form, which will colour everything for her. She will feel and know her own body very well too, and enjoy it, maybe very sexy and, again, will need to take care she doesn't use her attractiveness abusively or in an overly manipulative way. Her charisma will be strong, something she'll have to watch as with that many 1s she could easily have an ego the size of the planet! Now, this certainly does not need to be all bad, a strong ego makes a wonderful castle for the spirit to inhabit ... as long as she doesn't imprison it, like Rapunzel, with all the direful consequences of that tale.

Joanne will have to learn how to use the strengths which 1 to the power of 9 brings, and not to fall into the traps. Her worst pitfall will probably be a tendency to know best; the philosopher and psychologist CG Jung used to say to his students, "Never know best and never know first". This is an excellent dictum and one which Joanne should paste all over her bathroom mirror and engrave onto her heart.

With 6 as her birth number, *knowing* will be a force in her life which she'll need to get right, and it will be what she feels she's about ... and very strongly because of all those 1s, but the illusions cast by the bright light of her personal self will be a maze for her to find her way through. That goal of knowing, her birth number, will pull her very hard and she'll want to do it right, so she'll be full of the best intentions. –Best intentions are another disastrous quality and one of the most attractive traps for all of us; having 1 to the power of 9 is going to enhance that for Joanne nine-fold.

These are two of the major killers in human personalities – knowing best and good intentions. Good intentions come from a desire to do good, to help, cure all ills, stop all strife and suffering, create harmony in the world. They blind the person to the bigger picture. Knowing best compounds the problem of good intentions because the one who knows best will never think to ask the recipient of their generosity what they really need. The result is usually poison, physical, emotional and/or mental. Such an event actually occurred in India in the last century because the good-hearted persons didn't ask the people if they could actually eat wheat but assumed everyone can. Thousands of tons of wheat were sent to cover a famine. At that time the Indian population's stomachs were set to eat rice, the wheat bread they made caused terrible digestive problems If the philanthropists had asked, listened and heeded then the problem would not have occurred; the person who knows best has to overcome their inability to listen and take heed of what they are told. All of these are downsides of 1-ness which Joanne will have to overcome.

Joanne has 9 to the power of 3, and these three 9s put quite a reasonable counterweight on the nine 1s; they'll give her a strong call to use the power of the void through her thinking function, so she will come to understand it.

Joanne doesn't have to fall into the trap all those 1s have set for her. Her birth number makes her a 6-person, a potential wise owl, a knowing one. When she gets the hang of how to use her strong personal self to enable good rather than to do good she will be able to *know* successfully. Knowing, as we've seen when looking at 6-ness, has its own difficulties. It's unlikely Joanne will suffer from the absent-minded professor stuff with all those 1s but she could well inundate her audience with far too much information, and so lose them. the 1s will give her great enthusiasm and this will need careful driving so as not to get out of hand.

Joanne has one 6 – so she does her knowing with the flavour of 1-ness, and could be driven by it because she has so many 1s. 1-ness is about practicality, leadership, one-pointed-ness, focus and concentration. She will need to take not to become fixated in her knowing but always able to listen. She will be single-minded about whatever she does while she's doing it, her friends may need to encourage her to get a life beyond whatever her passion is. The old adage of *"work hard, play hard"* may fit Joanne but hopefully she won't become obsessive. The 1-ness flavour will ground her knowing and she has the ability to make it practical and real for others. Let's go through Joanne's numbers.

1-ness: 1 to the power of 9 gives Joanne a strong personal self and good grounding. She will love the body of the Earth and her own body with passion. The strength of her ability to identify with the planet could mean that she sense the pain of ecological damage within her own body. She will be a strong leader, single-minded and able to carry her projects through to completion. The strength of 1-ness will hold its own handicaps and Joanne will have to be aware of her own motivation in order to avoid them.

2-ness: Joanne has 2 to the power of 2 so she does her 2-ness with a two flavour. This gives her a strong feeling nature. She will be less likely to allow her feelings to rule than Anny would be because of the strength of her ego, the 1-ness. The 2s will help her empathise with those around her and be a leavening to the ego. She will need to take care she doesn't use her feelings, perhaps as tantrums, to manipulate others to suit her ego-drives.

3-ness: Joanne has one 3 so, again, she does 3-ness with the flavour of 1. Her thinking-self will be in tune with her ego-self which will help her reasoning powers. The drawback here is the tendency to push her thinking along the lines of the wants of the ego. It will be a subtle trap, well qualified by the "nosebest syndrome", knowing best, which she will have to see in herself before she can realign it. Once she has this under control her thinking will be a valuable tool to aid her in her spirit-job.

4-ness: Joanne has no 4s, this part of herself is hidden. When we come to her name you will see where she can find it.

5-ness: She has one 5, again she's working through the 1-ness filter, it is her natural way to finding her intuitive self, her job-description for this incarnation. She touches into the needs of the Plan through her earthly and earthy self, through the Earth herself – for Joanne all this will feel very similar. She may identify with the Earth, her ability to sense the planet's pain will accentuate this, her own cause will be the Earth's. There are dangers here, particularly of not being able to differentiate between things which happen to her and things which happene to the planet. She will need to use the strength of the 2-ness, the ability to recognise self and not-self, to get a handle on this.

6-ness: Joanne's birth number is 6. Inherently, she came into this incarnation to be a wise owl, a knowing one, but she set herself a serious task to do so. This probably means she-the-spirit really wants to get knowing into her spirit-bones this time around. We give our personalities a hard job when we really want to get something right. Joanne has the tools within her numbers to do a knowing-job very well, if she gets her act together.

7-ness: Joanne has no 7s. The Love/wisdom aspect of herself is hidden, she has to walk that pair from the personal self end, the 2-ness. Again, when we come to her name numbers you will see where she can find 7-ness.

8-ness: Her one 8 is the other half of her strong 1-ness, and she does 8-ness with a 1-flavour. This is her ancestral connection. Again she will need to be careful not to be autocratic in her dealings with the ancestors. But it also means she sees spirit through herself and does feel herself to be a part of it. There are two possible extremes here, first that she might feel everything is a part of herself rather than that she is a part of everything; and secondly she may feel unworthy, too ego-ridden and guilty to acknowledge she is a part of everything else. She may feel like a blot on the landscape. Neither of these two poles is useful either to her or to Otherworld and Joanne needs to find a balance here.

9-ness: Joanne has 9 to the power of 2, she does her 9-ness through her feeling nature. This combination of the void-energy with the feelings self will be less easy for Joanne than it is for Anny. Joanne is not a 9-person and the chaos energies won't feel like home to her. Her strong 1-ness can be the antipathy to chaos becoming an extreme need for order which, if threatened, will become rigidity. Where Anny find the void attractive, Joanne will be repelled. Seeing it through the emotional/feelings lens will exacerbate this. 9-ness will feel cold and inhuman which, of course, it is, although its inhumanity is not evil or nasty. Perhaps un-human would be a better word, not human. Joanne will find it very difficult to make or understand this distinction.

She will feel the power of 9-ness and, through the feelings-lens, may be tempted to emotional blackmail, to use her feelings to sway people into doing what she wants, perhaps by making them feel guilty. Her thinking self will be able to find reasonable arguments, weasel words, to support her emotional case and she will back that with the power from her 9-ness. A subtle and difficult pitfall.

0-ness: Joanne has zero to the power of 1 too, so Joanne does her mirroring with a 1-ness flavour. This could very well be blunt and autocratic, so making it very hard for her listener to hear the truth from her, and so defeating her own purpose. Joanne will need to work on this, again there are things in her name which will help.

Joanne's Name

Joanne's name adds down to 3, so her name number is 3 ...

J	O	A	N	N	E		D	O	N	N	E
1	6	1	5	5	5		4	6	5	5	5

Figure 55 Joanne name

1+6+1+5+5+5= 23 = 5   4+6+5+5+5= 25 = 7   5+7 = 12 = 3

So her name number is 3.

J	O	A	N	N	E	D	O	N	N	E
1	6	1	5	5	5	4	6	5	5	5

$$23$$
$$(2+3)$$
$$5$$

$$25$$
$$(2+5)$$
$$7$$

$$(5+7)$$
$$12$$
$$(1+2)$$
$$3$$

Figure 56 Joanne name numbers

Joanne gives herself two of the numbers she lacked in her birth chart – the 4 and the 7 – through her name, but she still has a tendency to excess as shown through the seven 5s.

When we put her birth and name numbers side by side it shows us a new picture of Joanne.

Name					Birth			
		0			^{3000}	0		
		9			^{299}	9		
-	8	1	11^2		8	8	1	1111111111^9
7	7	2	2		-	7	2	22
^{266}	6	3	3		6	6	3	3
^{75555555}	5	4	4		5	5	4	-

Figure 57 Joanne birth & name grids

First thing to note is that Joanne has given herself a whacking great dollop of seven 5s in her name; this will help balance out the enormous number of 1s in her birth grid.

She's also given herself the 4 and the 7 she lacked in her birth numbers; along with an extra 2, two extra 6s, and another 3.

Putting the birth and name numbers together gives us ...

^{3}000	0		
^{2}99	9		
8	8	1	11111111111^{11}
7	7	2	222^3
^{3}666	6	3	33^2
^{8}55555555	5	4	4

Figure 58 Joanne birth + name grid

She's still a woman who *needs* excess but the addition of the name numbers really does help her balance out the weighty off-centre balance of her birth numbers, she will be far less pulled into her personal self, and possibly over-blown ego, now. And her strong personal self (1) will be able to contain the very powerful intuitive qualities (5) she's now given herself. All this will help her sense into the job she designed for this lifetime.

So, let's go through her numbers now we've added the name to the birth.

1-ness: Joanne now has eleven 1s. This is enormous. She'll be someone you cannot help but notice wherever she is and this may well be a trial for her, as well as possibly for those around her. It gives her massive leadership skills, and a lot of charisma but, as always, she'll need to take care not to fall into the traps with which those traits will litter her path.

The problems here are those of knowing best and having good intentions which we've already discussed. Her spirit self has obviously decided that these traits can be useful for her and probably that she needs to learn to handle them well during this lifetime; this may also be "work for the future", preparation for a future lifetime too, not just work for this one. Our lives are huge great long threads which spiral round and around, ensuring we learn more in both breadth and depth in each incarnation, and that the traits we've already worked with can be honed further in future incarnations. I strongly suspect this is what's happening with Joanne.

Having a personal self that is as powerful as this one is a big job. It will make her hard to live with, and hard to work with as well. The charisma will help but don't forget it can be used as an enchantment which can disable the people around her rather than enable them.

2-ness: Having three 2s means she has a strong ability to feel provided she keeps it to feeling and doesn't confuse it with her thinking self. Joanne, with the aid of her name, now uses the 3-lens (thinking self) to focus her feeling-self. this can give her a tendency to *think* about feeling rather than feeling it, remember the old phrase "I think I feel ..."? Well which, Joanne? Are you thinking about feeling rather than doing it? That's no use at all, and gives you a completely useless approach to working with your feelings. On the good side though, it can help her achieve some detachment from her feelings and perhaps not be overwhelmed by them – having 2 to the power of 3 is quite a strong dose. She needs to bring her wise owl (6) in here to help as we'll see shortly.

3-ness: Conversely, Joanne uses her feeling self to focus on her thinking; this may compound the difficulties with working with her feelings as it sort of turns them upside-down. She really is going to need to work on this so she knows when she is feeling and when she is thinking. Giving herself this conundrum is a good way of getting herself into such a muddle she absolutely has to sort it out.

Mixing thinking and feeling like this really can land you with a problem which feels like a pile of knitting wool after a kitten has been playing with it. You can spend years disentangling it, and you need to know both these functions in your bones rather than from book-learned definitions. Joanne will spend years of sit-with, asking and listening, to work this out but it will be so worthwhile, she may also need outside help with it from someone who understands the difficulty, like a good counsellor or psychotherapist.

4-ness: Joanne gains a 4 from her name number which she didn't have in her birth numbers. This helps her get a handle on her instincts, help her get a handle on that big wadge of 5s she's given herself and so find her way to knowing her intuitive-self. Instincts, once she learns to know and trust them, will also help her understand when her ego gets out of hand and so gets in the way of what she wants to do. Knowing your own instincts helps you feel into those of others, and not just humans, so you can see what's going on, see how they see you, how you are perceived by others.

5-ness: Woof! Well she's certainly gone overboard with her 5s, and all for good reasons I'm sure. Through her name, her intuition, her 5-ness, is intensified to the power of 8. Now 8 is the number of spirit and the ancestral realms so Joanne has chosen to work with her intuition through them. It will be a major task but one sparkling with possibilities; the intuitive self is so close to spirit, and can be so well able to contact and work with the ancestors. A major task but exciting and full of challenges. Once she begins this she will find her life changes for the better straight away; once she has her intuition somewhat sorted, she could become a person who can really help others with their own paths. She will need to be careful of her personal self though, as that may lure her into becoming a guru in the sense of someone who can hold power over others – not a good path.

6-ness: Joanne now has three 6s, so she works her wise owl through her thinking self. As she also works her feeling self through thinking the 3-ness of the wise olw will be helpful in both cases. The wise owl is well able – as the partner of 3 – to work with the thinking self and to help thinking become the useful tool rather than the dominant function that modern life has made it. Thinking is now the prized function and has been for several centuries in what we call the civilised world, consequently the other functions get underused and tend to become atrophied. The wise owl can help right this and bring our other functions back to their rightful places.

7-ness: through her name, Joanne gives herself her access to love-wisdom; this is really good as she does it from her own choice, from choosing her own name. She's given herself just the one 7, so she's seeing it through her personal self and this will give her some challenges as she now has eleven 1s to contend with as well as to learn how to work successfully with. The addition of the 7-ness, the love wisdom, will ease her path here. It will also heighten her perception of self-ness, it may also enable her to still love herself even when she sees she's made some frightful ego-blunder. If she can do this then she has real possibilities of making good from making a mistake. Sitting around beating yourself up for making a mistake is about as useful as an ashtray on a motorbike (quote from my husband!), so just try not to go there.

8-ness: Joanne has just the one 8, so she's working her spirit and ancestral connections through her personal self and yes, of course, all those 1s will be both a hindrance and a blessing. The spirit realm is very strong, and so are the ancestors, but they will never force Joanne to work their way, her personal self must choose to do so at every turn. Having that 8 really is a help, even though there's only the one, the power of 8-ness can work subtly but is always very strong.

9-ness: Joanne has two 9s, so she works with the power of the void through her feeling self. If she goes for this it will help her greatly with seeing her feeling self through the lens of thinking, and conversely with using her thinking self through the lens of feeling. As I've said, the void is weird and difficult stuff, the power of black holes, but this power will help if we learn to use it and the feeling self is the softest way to do this.

With Joanne's problem of confusing thinking and feeling, using the 9-ness, the power of the void, will really set the cat amongst the pigeons; it will force her to see clearly but very possibly through tough tests and hard choices. Joanne's strong personality will help her through these.

0-ness: Joanne has three zeros, 0s. Her mirroring abilities will come through her thinking self and this could make them very sharp and pointed! Her repartee, ability to counter arguments and criticism could well be quite scathing and because of her strong personality she won't wish to hold back from such comments. Using the 3-ness of the wise owl, 6-ness, will help here. If she can combine this with her strong 5-ness (intuition) and her instincts which are focused through 1-ness then she will find a way to express herself, and mirror back to others, in a way which they can hear and see. If she just goes for it, without incorporating these qualities, she'll likely flay her companions alive!

Joanne's birth number, chosen by her spirit, is 6, the wise owl, while her name number gives her its pair, 3. This means that her birth number and her name number together make a whole, a 9. This is very powerful. If she works the two, birth and name, together she will certainly achieve the job she and her tylwyth set for this incarnation.

As we've seen, Joanne tends to extremes but it seems she needs them in order to be Joanne. Modern new age philosophies can suggest people shouldn't have extremes, excesses, that it's somehow not spiritual, but this is a gross simplification. It puts people in boxes which are not their size and shape. Remember balance isn't necessarily equal-sided, and that equal-sided balance is static – you cannot walk forward without going out of the equal balance of standing squarely on two feet. Remind yourself of this now, try walking without going out of balance to make the first (and following) steps.

Joanne is still a young woman as I write this in 2018. She needs lots more life-experience, to make mistakes, feel both joy and pain, fall in love and be rejected, have wonderful relationships, build and grow her garden spiritually and physically. All this will come. Her strong, independent, and possibly bolshie, personal self will help her gain all this life-experience, while her numbers give her the tools to learn from it. She's needed, and may still need, her strong self to make sure she lives her own life and doesn't try to live from other people's scripts. This way she can become a wise owl and, one day, have a huge trunk-full of experience and memories, so she can invite other folk into her attic to explore them and find useful things for themselves.

Joanne and Anny are two very different people. Both are powerful, but in their own ways. There's no right or wrong here. It's unwise to think of some numbers as being more spiritual than others and so more worth having, that's *either/or* thinking and so contrary to the way the universe works. We all have many incarnations, each with different purposes both for our own growth and how we can be useful to the cosmos. We take on different characteristics to suit each life and to give us traits which will be useful even if, at the time, we cannot see how. We are all part of the one whole, different and individual, and necessary.

Exercises to help you work with the numbers

Body-Knowing

Body-knowing is a technique humans have been pushing aside for a very long time in the belief that the mind is the place of knowledge. While the mind does hold knowledge, and some ways of how to learn and discover things intellectually, the mind doesn't know how to *know*. Every child has this ancient, inherent technique of *knowing*, until it's educated out of them by parents, teachers, friends, employers, peer groups and philosophies that try to make them conform and be normal.

Every animal still knows and works with body-knowing. But what is it?

Think about a tree. Now, imagine telling someone from another planet what tree-ness is ... not what a tree looks like, not what it's made of, not what species it is, not where it grows, but what it is to *be* a tree. And think about it when they ask you what is the difference between a tree and a bush. You know that inherently, but how do you tell them?

Try it now in imagination, as a thought experiment, try to tell ET what tree-ness is. No analogies, no pictures, no 'it's like a bush but bigger'. You have to *tell*, not show. Just about impossible?

But you *know*, intrinsically, what a tree is. You can recognise one. You'd probably have to resort to taking your extra-terrestrial friend out and showing them a tree, letting them touch the tree, smell it, hear its branches rustle, perhaps even taste it.

And that's part of the point! Notice, you resorted to the five bodily senses to get over what tree-ness is to ET?

You can use this method to know anything, and it's extremely effective. Once your body knows something you won't forget it, it'll be there, always, and will come back to you instantly whenever you need it ... unlike your thinking-memory which

153

often fails just at the inopportune moment.

An initial concept to take on board is that *everything* has life, spirit and consciousness. Intellectuals call this "animism". Anima is a word for breath, for spirit, so animism is about knowing the spirit in everything. As far as archaeologists can see it was the original ethos for human beings; they say evidence seems to support the idea that we all knew that all things have spirit … long, long ago. This idea has been shredded by just about all the religions that came after, they often wish to make human beings the most important thing in creation; saying that only humans have spirits is one way of doing this. These religions have further enforced uniformity by threats of dire punishment, in this world and any others, to those who don't believe as they're told to do. All of which has had unfortunate consequences on human attitudes to, and treatment of, all the life with whom we share this planet. The cruelty human-centeredness has spawned ranges through environmental stupidity, global warming, genetic engineering, agribusiness, cheap food, over-population … the list is pretty long. So animism, knowing the spirit in all things, can head us away from causing quite so much damage to our planet.

It can also help enormously with knowing yourself. Every cell in your body has a consciousness and a memory. It is both an individual cell *and* an essential member of a group. The cell is itself and part of an organ in your body at the same time. Your body too is an entity in its own right. As you know, it was created by your spirit as a home for this incarnation, and it was built out of the stuff, the matter, of this planet, which stuff you will return to the planet when your spirit leaves this incarnation and your body dies. Every atom, every tiniest piece of matter which makes up your body, has consciousness, and that consciousness holds the knowledge and memory of everything that has happened to it. That knowing might even stretch back the 4.5 billion years since the Earth grew herself out cosmic dust clouds and supernovae, maybe even back into the supernova itself.

All your experiences from birth to death are recorded in your cells' memory. Unsophisticated people (i.e. non-head-sets), animals and children have natural access to this, they still know how to listen to this memory and information. You have experienced the insights you can gain through the simple exercise of drawing the numbers themselves, which helps show you what the body-actions of drawing give you.

The best and simplest way of accessing body knowing is to ASK the body for it but, for most of us, this requires letting go of a whole raft of preconceptions. Many, if not all, of these support our current self and world view, our current reality, and our intellect is terrified of letting go of them ... if we do, the world might well fall apart! That fear, lurking at the back of our brains, is one of the best stops for beginning the process of asking. Another fear is that we will look stupid, people will laugh at us, if we are even thought to be asking our body what it thinks of us changing our job or taking a lover. All of these are huge hurdles in the way of listening to our body-knowing.

So how do you learn to about body-knowing and asking the body?

Many people have found the following exercise very effective as a beginning.

Body-Knowing Exercise

Take a piece of paper and write Body on it.

Have enough space to lie down in.

Sit quietly and clear yourself of worries and thoughts, allow them to flow past you, like having the TV on but not watching it. Find yourself at a still point.

When you are ready, lie down. Settle into that place, feel yourself within your body, feel connected with it.

Ask Body, does it have anything it wishes to tell you? Any advice, words, phrases, pictures, senses, scents, images, gifts, for you? Spend the next fifteen minutes listening and hearing what Body it has to say to you. Attend to Body.

As the time comes to a close, thank Body for being with you, for what it has told and given you. Accept any gifts.

Say [and mean it] that you will return to listen to Body again soon.

Say farewell.

When you are ready sit up gently. Clear your thoughts and bring yourself back to your everyday consciousness. Make brief drawings, notes, reminders, of what Body said to you and gave you.

When you are ready get up and clear your space. Keep your notes tidy somewhere, get yourself a cup of tea and sit and look over them while you remember the experience. Don't spend too long on this. Then put them away until tomorrow and do something completely different.

I modify this exercise for all sorts of purposes and you'll find a couple of them later on, but this is a good way of beginning to listen to your body-knowing.

You've now experienced listening to your body, asking it to tell you, show you, what it knows. Body often speaks to us through sensations, scents, feelings in our bones, or our water as the old adage has it, scalp prickling, feeling weak at the knees or light-headed. You can call up the old sayings on Google to understand better what they say. Your body gives you have an inkling of how came about, so you can begin to re-member them for yourself.

Next day, take the notes you made in the first Body Exercise and spend time with them. Do this in an easy way, curled on the sofa maybe, with your favourite drink. Be alone. Resist any temptation you have to tell your friends and loved ones about your experience. Don't talk about it; this sort of experience needs time to brew, to ferment, to distil. It's like its counterpart, the physical spirit of an old brandy, cognac, a single malt whisky.

Don't hurry it, don't open the vat and stir it, don't try to pour it for your friend until it's aged suitably. Remember the farmer and his onions – the story goes that the farmer was very worried whether his onions were growing, so he went round the whole field pulling them up to see if they were! We just don't need to do that.

So take your notes and ponder them in luxurious solitude. Pondering is another spiritual technique worth learning. To do it properly you have to send your intellect and your reasoning powers out to play for an hour or so. If you keep them with you they will wreck the whole process and you'll end up even more befuddled by reason than when you started out. Give your intellect and reasoning powers some virtual pocket money and send them off to play.

Set yourself up in a favourite, comfortable place, with your favourite drink, paper, coloured pencils/crayons and put the "Do not disturb" sign on the door. When you're sitting comfortably, pick up your notes from the first Body Exercise and just hold them. Close your eyes so you can't be tempted to begin reading them.

You'll receive sensations in your body again. It might be as simple as hearing your heart beat, or your breathing. Whatever sensation you notice as you hold your notes, allow it to seep into you, go through you. Mentally note any images, words or phrases which come, or any apparent changes of light noticeable through your *closed* eyelids. There will come a moment when the experience "switches off". When this happens put the notes down and open your eyes.

Have a sip of that drink.

Using your coloured pens/crayons, make a new set of drawings and notes to remind you of the sensations you've just experienced. Write the words in colour too. Deliberately, don't be neat, write words sideways and upside-down all over the paper. Let your hand choose where and how to draw and write.

If you're right handed try letting your left hand do the drawing, and the writing. If you're left handed let your right hand do it. You are re-educating yourself to understanding when your body talks to you instead of dismissing it as an aberration as we are so encouraged to do nowadays.

When you've got your latest set of notes down on paper, pick up your first set and look at them. Try not to read at first, just look. It should be easier because you've woken and worked with your body, that's why I asked you to do those exercises *before* reading your notes. It's a way of getting your normal brain to go off-line, so freeing up space for your body to come on-line. *Have another sip of that drink!*

Look at your first set of notes, what patterns do you see in them?

When you've got an idea of this, take the second set of notes and look at them. What patterns do you see? And what similarities are there in the patterns from the two sets of notes?

Take a third piece of paper and draw/write (in colour) the similarities you just found. Draw their pattern. Write their words. Then sit sipping that drink and contemplate this third set of patterns. Insights will come to you; as they do, roll their names, the words for them, around your mouth like a piece of delicious chocolate. Words, and the insights they carry are as delicious as this. Savour them.

You can savour ideas and concepts like good food or a beautiful perfume. 'Nutrition of the senses', as Rudolph Steiner put it, although he didn't go quite as far as you and I are doing. By savouring, feeding your senses, you are putting all that experience into your cell-memory. Doing this, allowing yourself to be this intense in the work, enhances your experience so you're able to go back to your body and get a very realistic action-replay.

This is body-knowing.

Earth/Sun Exercise

Try to do this exercise every day when you get up and when you go to sleep at night; it will help your dreaming and recall. You can do the exercise sitting or standing. It's very good if, at first, you can do it outside and with bare feet, but this isn't always possible.

Read the script through several times so you get to know what you're going to do. Do the exercise standing up at first, as this helps you to feel it through your body.

Stand or sit relaxed, weight evenly distributed.

Make sure your back is *comfortably* straight, neither rigid nor in spasm. Forearms, wrists, hands, relaxed. Neck and head comfortable, with a slight forward tilt to allow the energy to pass *down and up* your spine easily. You need to anchor to the Earth before you reach out to the Sun.

Now ... focus on your breathing, just allow the breath to flow in and out without any changes. This quiets you, helps take you out of your head-space.

When you feel quiet ... imagine the heart of the Earth beneath you, the heart of the Sun above you and your own heart at the centre.

See a thread of energy go *down* out of your heart centre, down the spine, down through the ground, down to the central fire at the *heart of the Earth*.

See the thread of energy penetrate this fire at the *heart of the Earth* and be lit by a spark there.

Now ... see that spark, from the heart of the Earth, travel back *up* your thread, through the earth, through the ground, up the spine and out through the top of your head.

See the spark from the Heart of the Earth travelling *up* through space, until it reaches the heart of the Sun. See it enter the Sun.

See the Earth-fire and the Sun-fire meet and greet each other, see them join together.

Now ... Earth-fire leads Sun-fire back *down* your thread, across space, through your crown, down the spine and down to the heart of the Earth.

Sun-fire grows brighter.

Now ... they turn, Sun-fire leads Earth-fire back *up* through your spine, through your crown, across space and into the heart of the Sun.

Earth-fire grows brighter.

Now ... they turn again, Earth-fire leads Sun-fire back *down* across space, through your crown, through your spine, and into the heart of the Earth.

They dance, up and down, down and up. Each grows brighter with every passage.

Spend time watching the conjoined sparks journey between the heart of the Earth and the heart of the Sun.

Now ... this time ... as they arrive again in the Sun, see the pulsing movement gently slow and stop as the Earth-spark and Sun-spark kiss and part company.

The Sun-spark retires back into the heart of the Sun and the Earth-spark flows back down your spine, through you and into the heart of the Earth where it gently leaves go of your thread and retires into the smouldering fire.

Now ... gently withdraw your thread from the heart of the Sun. See, feel, the thread roll back down into your crown, down your spine, to curl into your heart.

Now ... gently withdraw your thread from the heart of the Earth. See, feel, the thread roll back up into your body, up your spine, to curl into your heart.

Feel yourself disengage from Otherworld, back in your everyday-self.

Feel the ground beneath you, reach down and touch it, rub your hands on it. Rub your knees, your feet, then rub your hands together. Rub your body, arms, legs, neck, head. Roll your head on your neck. Yawn. Breathe deeply in, then blow the breath out

160

hard, do this again … and again. Roll your tongue around your mouth, lick your lips. Open your eyes, roll your eyes around and focus on something near, then something further off. Roll your shoulders. Stretch your arms. Arch your back then bend forward. Finally slide onto the ground and lie in the foetal position for a few minutes, reconnecting with the Earth.

Know yourself to be here … and know where here is.

Now you've done the exercise go eat, drink and give yourself some treats. Then, when you feel ready, make drawings and notes, look back over the exercise.

This exercise underpins all your work. Try to make it a daily habit. It's *very* grounding; it will anchor you to the Earth and – at the same time – enable you to reach out across the Solar System to the sun whose light and warmth enable life on Earth. It will help you *know* all creation through your own body, know it in your bones.

Sun Glyph Exercise

This is the glyph of the sun; a dot at the centre of a circle.

Figure 59 Sun glyph

This exercise which will help you experience and learn more about the universe.

Sit or lie quietly. Become aware of your breathing. Don't try to change anything, just hear and feel the movement of air into and out of your body, feel your lungs work as they suck air in and blow it out again.

The rhythm is hypnotic and you may find it slows down as you become accustomed to it. Allow the rhythm to transport you.

Find yourself out in space, in the velvety blackness of space surrounded by a myriad of beautiful stars, like diamonds on velvet.

Feel yourself to be a point of light, like a star. Feel yourself becoming infinitely small and yet you're always there. The smaller you become the more intense is your sense of being.

Now, allow yourself to expand. You become bigger and bigger until you encompass the whole universe. Your sense of being-ness is now as fine as gossamer and yet still as strong as steel.

Contract again, become a pinpoint of light. Expand again and become the whole universe. Spend a little time moving between these two states.

Come to a place of stillness, try holding both concepts within you, so you are *both* infinitely small and infinitely huge at the same time. You are both, and one. You are a point of light within a greater light.

Be still there. Allow the sensations to flow through you. Don't try to analyse, just BE.

When you are ready, allow yourself to come back to body-consciousness. Bring yourself back from space, come back to earth, your home. Feel yourself within your body again.

Become aware of your breathing again, follow its rhythm. This time, allow it to bring you back home to your body again.

As you become aware of your body again you may find it actually feels big. This is OK. You are, in fact, physically sensing your etheric body which you're usually unaware of. That *is* bigger than your physical body, so you're sensing reality. Don't worry, begin to move your fingers and toes. At first that might seem a bit difficult, but just keep on doing it, gradually your awareness will return to its usual state where you are primarily conscious of your physical body.

What happened in the exercise?
You *became* the glyph, the dot within the circle.

You knew yourself to be a point of light within the whole universe and you also became that whole universe.

You now have a body-knowing of the power of creation.

As I told at the beginning, in the chapter on Duality, I first found myself doing this when I went to bed, when I was a wee kiddie (about 5 or 6). I found it utterly thrilling and still do, so I was easy to get to bed. Dad asked me why I was so keen to go to bed so I told him, he then explained it back to me in very baby-steps; he could be a good lad, my dad.

This is part of the being everything that Taliesin talks of in his poem; this takes you right out beyond space-time as we know it and into the width and depth of the universe. It's a really wonderful journey.

This is Taliesin's (or Amergin's in Gaelic) famous song about "I am Everything".

> *I am a stag: of seven tines,*
> *I am a flood: across a plain,*
> *I am a wind: on a deep lake,*
> *I am a tear: the Sun lets fall,*
> *I am a hawk: above the cliff,*
> *I am a thorn: beneath the nail,*
> *I am a wonder: among flowers,*
> *I am a wizard: who but I*
> *Sets the cool head aflame with smoke?*
> *I am a spear: that roars for blood,*
> *I am a salmon: in a pool,*
> *I am a lure: from paradise,*

I am a hill: where poets walk,
I am a boar: ruthless and red,
I am a breaker: threatening doom,
I am a tide: that drags to death,
I am an infant: who but I
Peeps from the unhewn dolmen, arch?
I am the womb: of every holt,
I am the blaze: on every hill,
I am the queen: of every hive,
I am the shield: for every head,
I am the tomb: of every hope.
Song of Amergin translated by Robert Graves, from **The White Goddess**, Faber and Faber Limited, 24 Russell Square London WC1. *It appears here under the principle of Fair Use.*

Exercise: Contacting Your Spirit

Make a space for yourself where you won't be disturbed for an hour. It's good to make an offering to the four elements which make up life on this planet – earth, air, fire and water. Use a small pot of soil from your garden or plant pot for the earth, water from your tap for the water element, scented flowers for air, and a candle for fire.

In focused meditations like this it's important to retain discipline. Your actual journey should be only about twenty minutes. For this purpose, I suggest you sit in a comfortable chair which supports your back, your muscles should be able to relax but you don't go to sleep. Again, don't do this work when you're tired, you need to be fresh and awake, it's a conscious consciousness process, not a dream.

Get yourself a glass of water, paper, pens, crayons, tissues (in case tears come or your nose needs blowing). Make sure you're warm and comfortable. Put a "do not disturb" notice on the door and turn of the phones. Put a clock where you can see it when you come back. Make sure no bright light or sunlight will hit your eyes and disturb you.

As you do this, compose yourself and say aloud ...

I am ready to meet my spirit
I am ready to meet my spirit
I am ready to meet my spirit
Spirit, I invite you to come in

Then sit back comfortably in your chair and close your eyes.

Wait. Don't panic. Wait quietly and watchfully.

Observe every feeling and sensation in your body.

Be aware of your breathing and follow its rhythm.

Allow your excitement to calm down.

Your spirit will come. It may or may not look like you expect it to. It will be wearing an appearance as you wear clothes, so that you will recognise and respond to it. The images and memories which its appearance brings to mind are important. Your spirit is using these as part of its means of communication with you.

When your spirit comes, ask it ... *"Are you my spirit?"*.

Ask three times, so you are sure. Spirit always gives you the true answer on the third asking; the old stories show you this principle.

Part of growing up spiritually is to learn not to go blindly galumphing off with the first Otherworld being who shows up. It's quite possible Otherworld will test you this way, and you should take it as a compliment if they do. It means they think you're growing up and so are worthy of testing. Your spirit, too, will be pleased to see you ask.

When you know it is your spirit ask it what it needs of you, right now, at this time.

Don't begin with a shopping list of your wants nor a life-story of your joy and grief. Remember, your spirit already knows all this. Adults ask the visitor what they need and put their personal wants on hold while they listen attentively. If you do this you'll be amazed to find that what your spirit tells you will assuage your personal needs, and in ways you'd not even considered.

So listen to your spirit.

You will probably be asked if you really mean it that you are ready, and if you are willing for your spirit to be in conscious contact with you every day now. Answer from your heart. Don't try to think of "right answers", that's the child's way not the adult's.

Your spirit will, of course, know you are reading about Numerology so ask if it will help you to use this tool as means of growth. Have a conversation with your spirit.

When the conversation draws to a close, thank your spirit for coming and ask if it will now come and live in your conscious personal-self. If it says yes then work out between you how to do this. When you've got it, this will probably happen instantaneously. Don't assume the spirit will come to live with you, ask, be polite.

Return to your everyday consciousness, in your own room. It's good to stretch, rub your hands, arms, legs, head, to remind yourself of your physical body and ensure your consciousness is within it again. Have a drink of water. Now, before anything else, draw, write words, to remind yourself of what happened, what you saw and, most particularly, what your spirit told you. Drawings are much better reminders than words.

When you're done drawing and writing, close the elements altar. Blow out the candle, saying thank you to the fire element; pour away the water, thanking the water element; breathe in the last of the scent and thank the flowers for the air element; put the soil back where it came from. This tidying process helps to put a boundary, an edge, on your journey so you don't have bits of it drifting about with you all over the place like an old cobweb.

Put your drawings and notes aside, look at them again tomorrow. For now, let your journey go into the Cauldron of the Unconscious, to brew.

Go over your notes each day, in a quiet moment over a cup of tea. Add to them as they draw more images, words and phrases out of your mind. This is a process of getting to know yourself better, and your spirit, joining them up as a working team.

Repeat this exercise in a few days. This time change your invocation to ...

I would like to speak with my spirit
I would like to speak with my spirit
I would like to speak with my spirit

You still need to check, each time, that it is your spirit who comes, don't be sloppy about this discipline. Over a period, which may take months, you'll become accustomed to your spirit and, gradually, you'll find it feels natural and normal. In time, and don't rush it, you will find yourself ready to do the next exercise – moving to the seat of the spirit.

Exercise: Sitting in the Seat of Your Spirit

Choose two chairs in your room, not side by side but at an angle so you can see the other chair from the on you're sitting in without turning the head, but not face to face.

Make sure you won't be disturbed for half an hour.

Have pens and paper to record the experience.

Have water to drink and tissues in case you need them.

Do the Earth/Sun

Sit in one of the chairs – it doesn't matter which – quiet yourself, watch your breathing, feel it slow, feel yourself becoming still, focused, alert.

Say to yourself, out loud, ... *I am sitting in the seat of the personality*

Sense, feel, how this is for you.

Have your eyes open, look at the room, take in how the room looks from *this* perspective, sitting in *this* chair.

When you feel you have got a good sense of being in this

place, withdraw your attention from the room. Make sure you feel alert.

Get up from this chair and move to sit in the other.

Quiet yourself again, watch your breathing, feel yourself become still, focused and alert.

Say to yourself ... *I am sitting in the seat of the spirit*

Sense, feel, how this is for you.

Have your eyes open, look at the room, take in how the room looks from this perspective, sitting in this chair.

Note how this feels different from the other chair.

When you're ready, re-focus and clear yourself. This time say out loud, *I am leaving the seat of the soul to return to the seat of the personality*

Get up and move back to the other seat, then say ... *I am sitting in the seat of the personality*

Sense, feel, what this is like now.

Note to yourself how it is different from being in the seat of the spirit. When you feel it's right, say ... *I am leaving the seat of the personality to return to the seat of the soul* and get up and move to the other chair.

Repeat this sequence of sitting in each seat 3 times.

Clear yourself of the exercise, make sure you are back to your everyday self, awake and aware, back in your normal time and space. Doodle-draw some reminders of what happened.

Tidy things away, get yourself a drink and a piece of cake. Do this exercise several times.

Your spirit-self needs stretching and growing too, it isn't, never was and never will be "perfect"; perfect means there's nowhere to go, stuck, stationary and effectively dead. Your spirit grows all the time, that's why it chooses nice, challenging incarnations.

Torch Exercise

The torch exercise will show you about 3-ness, 4-ness and 7-ness

168

but it does take a while to fathom it all out. Do the exercise, watch what happens at each stage, then put the whole thing into your mind-cauldron and allow it to brew. Over time, you'll find more and more correlations, threads of knowing, come together and gradually make sense for you. It's a *consciousness-changing* exercise so do it, don't just read about it.

You need ...

1 **red**, 1 **blue** and 1 **green** LED torch; you're going to use 3 light-sources that each create a *spot* of light on the wall.

A white wall or other uncoloured surface to project onto.

Now, set each of the LED lights to point at the same spot on the wall. Each light must cover the other, this is important, spend time on it, if the lights don't overlap you won't get the effect.

Begin with the red LED, then focus the green one so it exactly covers the red ... watch the colour change. Now focus the blue one over the combined red and green LEDs ... what happens?

You now have white light on the spot where you began with a spot of red light, changed its colour by adding green, and by adding the blue you have white light.

So, adding red light to green light and to blue light makes white light.

This is the reverse of Newton's prism experiment, where he split white light through a prism.

Hopefully this is setting off ideas in your head about 3-ness; the 3 worlds, Upperworld, Lowerworld and Middleworld and how they all come together to make the whole. Other 3-ness ideas might be maiden-mother-crone, and again how they come together to make the whole. This 3-ness which comes together to make 1-ness is fundamental to many (perhaps most) shamanic traditions all around the world.

Here's a table of 3-ness correlations to ponder on ...

Earth	You	Sun
Mother	Child	Father
Poet	Healer	Blacksmith
Past	Present	Future
Ancestors	Actuality	Inspiration
Lowerworld	Middleworld	Upperworld

Figure 60: 3-ness table

Sit-with this table and allow yourself to *doodle* more correspondences. Remember *doodle*, don't write neatly, scribble, draw things, link them up with lines, do mind-maps; doing that allows your instincts and intuition to come out to play and puts your thinking-brain on the back burner. That's a very important habit to learn, using your mind to figure out everything stultifies all your other abilities and stops you learning.

OK, back to the torch exercise. As you set the LEDs up you watched the colours change so that, when all 3 were set you had a spot of white light on the wall. Now, make sure they're all still aligned correctly so you still have that white spot on the wall, then pass your hand between the torches and the wall ...

What happens on the wall?

What happens on your hand?

Watch the rainbow shadows of colour on your hand and on the wall, do it several times so the concept begins to go into your bones even if you don't yet understand it with your brain. Your brain will eventually catch up, but the important thing is to get it into your bones, into your instincts, then it can work with you successfully..

Our ancient ancestors understood this and used the symbol of the triskele all through the Celtic lands; we can now see it and come to understand it through light, through the composition of white light. Sir Albert Newton showed us this in his prism experiment, actually he showed it the other way around by splitting visible white light into its different colours, and showing us the rainbow. Humans have used the rainbow as part of their philosophy ever since they first saw it, now you can bring it into your consciousness in new ways. It helps you understand the world, the universe and everything and so how you, through your numbers, fit and work with the whole of the rest of the cosmos.

The Way Forward

Now you've walked the spiral path of the numbers with me you may well feel like getting your teeth deeper into the subject. It's fascinated me now for over sixty years, and it can lead you into lots of other things too.

Sometimes people in our modern world can become too compartmentalised and this precludes an awful lot of growth and development. It always seems a shame not to be curious, not to want to know more about the world, the universe and everything; curiosity about yourself, who you are, what got you here, and what your purpose is, all help you learn and understand more about everything else too.

Like learning about stars, learning about yourself takes you into both the past and the future. When we look up at the stars we may not realise how long their light has taken to reach us. Our nearest star, Alpha Centauri, is about four light years away, that means that her light has taken four whole Earth-years of time to get from her to us. So we're looking at that star as she was four years ago, not as she is in our now. Have a ponder on that.

Your own life is made up in part of your past, and of your ancestors' pasts too. We're all connected through those energy-threads that twine between us like the fungal mycorrhiza does between the plants. We sometimes call these energy-threads of life the deer trods here in Britain, meaning the footprints of our Mother Deer goddess, Elen of the Ways. Following the deer trods can lead you to the most amazing places and really expand your view of all of life, including the whole cosmos. The past helps to make the future, and they go on to bring about the future. Knowing this, and feeling it in your bones, helps you feel at home on the space-time thread of your life.

Getting a feel for the interconnectedness of all things, and of all lives, the past and the future, helps you get a better understanding of the vital importance of death in order that life can be. When you come to know this then your perspective on death changes, it's no longer a dreadful sword hanging over you, something you try not to think about and something you fear. It becomes a normal part of the whole process of living. You come to know that reincarnation of your spirit-self is how it has always been and always will be. And not only for you but for all your loved ones too, your family, friends, the animals that share your life; they're not gone forever when their physical bodies give up and go back to being atoms of the planet Earth again. No indeed, their spirits still live, and you can learn how to speak with them. And you can learn to speak with the spirits of place and of plants and animals, rocks and water and air, for everything has spirit, anima, and it's just waiting for us to notice and say "Hi".

So enjoy your future explorations of the wonderful universe we live in ... and thank your numbers for helping to show you the way in.

Moon Books

PAGANISM & SHAMANISM

What is Paganism? A religion, a spirituality, an alternative belief system, nature worship? You can find support for all these definitions (and many more) in dictionaries, encyclopaedias, and text books of religion, but subscribe to any one and the truth will evade you. Above all Paganism is a creative pursuit, an encounter with reality, an exploration of meaning and an expression of the soul. Druids, Heathens, Wiccans and others, all contribute their insights and literary riches to the Pagan tradition. Moon Books invites you to begin or to deepen your own encounter, right here, right now.

If you have enjoyed this book, why not tell other readers by posting a review on your preferred book site. Recent bestsellers from Moon Books are:

Journey to the Dark Goddess
How to Return to Your Soul
Jane Meredith
Discover the powerful secrets of the Dark Goddess and transform your depression, grief and pain into healing and integration.
Paperback: 978-1-84694-677-6 ebook: 978-1-78099-223-5

Shaman Pathways – The Druid Shaman
Exploring the Celtic Otherworld
Danu Forest
A practical guide to Celtic shamanism with exercises and
techniques as well as traditional lore for exploring the Celtic
Otherworld.
Paperback: 978-1-78099-615-8 ebook: 978-1-78099-616-5

Traditional Witchcraft for the Woods and Forests
A Witch's Guide to the Woodland with Guided Meditations and
Pathworking
Melusine Draco
A Witch's guide to walking alone in the woods, with guided
meditations and pathworking.
Paperback: 978-1-84694-803-9 ebook: 978-1-84694-804-6

Naming the Goddess
Trevor Greenfield
Naming the Goddess is written by over eighty adherents and
scholars of Goddess and Goddess Spirituality.
Paperback: 978-1-78279-476-9 ebook: 978-1-78279-475-2

Readers of ebooks can buy or view any of these bestsellers by clicking on the live link in the title. Most titles are published in paperback and as an ebook. Paperbacks are available in traditional bookshops. Both print and ebook formats are available online.

Find more titles and sign up to our readers' newsletter at
http://www.johnhuntpublishing.com/paganism
Follow us on Facebook at https://www.facebook.com/MoonBooks
and Twitter at https://twitter.com/MoonBooksJHP